# We Suffered Enough, Let Our Next Generation To Be Free

D1234106

## Ademir Souza

# Dedication

I dedicate this book to my wife, Maria Souza (Zeza), an exceptional woman. To my son, Davidson, my daughters, Natalia and Aline, because they understood that money doesn't grow on trees. Still, with hard work and God's blessings, everything is possible. All of them graduated from college, found their best partners for life, and gave me the most beautiful grandkids (Samuel, Sienna, Desmond, Kamila, (Ana Lucia, and Margareth). I also want to thank my family at www.blountfinefoods.com for their great support. I thank you guys from the bottom of my heart.

# Acknowledgments

I want to thank my teacher, Lucia Helena Alves Gaeta, who inspired me to think by myself and never let the media dictate what I should accept as the truth; always research, and I will find what matters. That teacher was my hero during high school in Brazil, and until today she is the one. Also, I want to thank my sister, Valdete Silva (Dete), who helped me in the dark period of my high school, paid for both of my colleges, stayed with me, supporting and encouraged me throughout my troubled days.

# About the Author

I am originally from Brazil, where I spent 30 good years of my life. When I was thirteen, the government took power into their hands so my country would not be a communist, which was very good.

My father came home every night to hear the news on the radio. I would be sitting in a corner, thinking, "What is the matter with us? What is happing right now in the politician's world?" My neighbor, one day, was arrested inside his own home because his son gave his name to the police, saying that he was assembling meetings to overcome the situation. We never heard about him anymore.

At 24 years old, I became a police officer myself, tried to do the right things, helped the traffic, helped the kids at school, and was a math tutor. But I felt that I did not have enough power to do as much as a simple soldier.

I went to the lieutenant academy, and after three years, when I was able to do my best, four months before my graduation day, I was fired from the force. Allegation? I was not fit for the uniform. At that time, I had the best record at the academy, and at the same time, I got the record to have more punishment in the school. Why is that? When I graduated, the authorities feared that I would pass my colleagues on promotion, and then they set up a trap. In one conference provided to us about drugs, the speaker gave us a sample of marijuana. In my packet came some seeds.

I was responsible for beautifying the academy in my spare time and collecting plants from our neighbors, and knowing that we had some officials that didn't know about the plant, I buried the seeds in a vase in front of the main door. It was beautiful.

I received some commandments from my friends, telling me how I had the guts to do that because many didn't even recognize the difference between street drugs from the beautiful plant.

BUT, six months later, the lieutenant, who was my commander, "discovered" the plant, and with that, I was disbarred from the force. What a shame! The force had lost its best man!

# Preface

After I was disbarred from the force, I became a mechanic teacher, discovering my real talents.

For eight years, I dealt with good and bad students, though they all loved me.

Finally, my dream to come to America resurfaced, and I couldn't stall it anymore.

In 1986, I arrived here; no money, no English, no goals. The only thing I knew was that I wanted to be here.

After six months, my family came, I had a job, and now I was happy. I worked hard, and my family grew. I had my opportunities, and my life was good.

BUT, as my heart was still suffering to see how my people were being manipulated, the schools that I loved so much were being destroyed, the kids in kindergarten being redirected by pernicious subjects, my Supreme Court being violated, the Senate being connivant, I decided to write this book. I wanted to tell my friends, students, and neighbors that we could reverse the situation. And here I am.

Thank you very much.

# Contents

Page Left Blank Intentionally

# Chapter 1: Communism

*"How do you tell a Communist? Well, it's someone who reads Marx and Lenin. And how do you tell an anti-Communist? It's someone who understands Marx and Lenin."* -**Ronald Reagan**

Ronald Reagan, the 40th President of America, meant that you would never support it if you truly understood what communism was. I believe in having faith in one political or economic theory and not in another, where one should interpret the system of ideas and ideals behind that theory. A deep understanding and study of any political theory can lead to better decision-making ability. Which, when not done right, can have catastrophic effects on a nation. Once you understand your nation's system, you will see all the flaws that lie behind it and what a political system conceals. Such an approach gives the people an opportunity to make the right decision for the future of their country instead of blindly following some so-called leaders and their malicious political agendas.

The more you learn, the better decision you will be able to take. Sadly, when the time came to make a decision that would have altered the fate of my country, Brazil, the people followed a system that had been around for ages than understanding the other option they always have – of democracy. The results of such faithful following can be seen today, what Brazil is now and where it stands. Yes, I am referring to the communist system that constructed Brazil and depleted a nation full of potential. Had communism been the best option, Brazil would not have faltered. You see, the impacts of communism along

1

with democracy in several regions of the world, including Brazil, are blurred. We need to understand what exactly communism is. We need to know how and when communism took over the control of the political and economic system in many significant countries of the world. We need to expand on the impact of communism and the basic idea behind it so that we can understand the depths of how this system has only made matters worse than what it promises – equality.

You must be curious why I am talking about communism so negatively. Well, there is a reason that I will share with you by the end of this chapter. Although, before I take you there, why don't I introduce you to what communism is and where it came from. When people bowed their heads to communism, they failed to grasp the idea behind it. I believe the root cause of people blindly following communism is their negligence and lack of knowledge. It will be futile anyway for me to be telling you about something that you do not know of. So, let's take a little detour before I lead you to the path of amendment where you redesign  your future by making the right choice when it comes to choosing  a fair political system.

## What is Communism?

Communism is both a political and economic system. In such a system, the factors of production are owned by a particular group. And when you talk about a country, that group is the government. The economic and political ideology of communism is opposite to that of capitalism and also liberal democracy. Hence, a communist raises a voice for a system not divided by social class or wealth. In such a system, entrepreneurship, natural resources, labor, and capital goods are the ways of production in the country. Moreover, these means of production are not at all privately owned. Hence, the group or community owns the means of production, and private property is almost non-existent.

Sadly, communism is still a state system of a few countries, and fortunately, many countries have completely or partially eliminated the communist approach in their governmental systems. Countries like Cuba, China, Laos, Vietnam, and North Korea are known as communist countries today. Previously, Armenia, Azerbaijan, Belarus, Estonia, Georgia, Kazakhstan, Kyrgyzstan, Latvia, Lithuania, Moldova, Russia, Tajikistan, Turkmenistan, Ukraine, Uzbekistan, Bulgaria, Czech Republic, East Germany, Hungary, Poland, Romania, and Slovakia were communist countries that were either part of the Soviet Union or Soviet-controlled Eastern bloc. Other than that, Afghanistan, Cambodia, Mongolia, Yemen, Albania, Bosnia and Herzegovina, Bulgaria, Croatia, Rep. of Macedonia, Montenegro, Serbia, Slovenia, Angola, Benin, Dem Rep. of Congo, Ethiopia, Somalia, Eritrea, and Mozambique were also communist countries in the past.

According to the Marxist theory, these communist countries of today are not entirely communist, as, in these countries, the supply is in the hands of the state. Hence, these countries are transforming from socialism where the supply is in the hands of the state rather than being decided by the laws of supply and demand. Here we need to understand the basic difference between the key terminologies like socialism, communism, capitalism, and fascism used for the political and economic ideologies.

Communism and socialism are mostly used interchangeably. Though they are closest in their practices and philosophy, in socialism, the product of the economy is distributed as per the ability. While in communism, it is the need that is put forth. Communism is also similar to fascism in terms of central plans. That is, a central authority takes the economic decisions. Communism and capitalism are opposite because, in capitalism, private owners control the country's trade and industry for profit rather than the state.

There are several layers of communism, which, I believe, are important to understand. To understand communism and its perception, especially by today's young generation, we need to dive deep into the minds of the biggest advocates of communism: Karl Marx and Vladimir Lenin. Let's look at the birthplace of communism.

## Where Did Communism Come from?

In the mid-19th century (1848–1849), Germany faced a major social uprising. The process of this revolution had begun in the 1840s. But it spiked in 1848, and protests broke out in other European countries. The states of the German Confederation encountered several rebellions. The main reason for this revolution was the discontent of the people in the autocratic political system. For a decade, people mainly belonging to the lower class faced difficulties due to halted economic progression and rationalization of the agricultural and industrial sectors. The working class was fighting unemployment and trying to improve their living conditions. This, along with the overthrow of the bourgeois King Louis-Philippe, eventually led to major unrest in Germany as the working class felt ignored and deprived. Consequently, this became the point when Marxism was born and widely supported.

## Marxism

Karl Heinrich Marx was German. He was born in Trier, Germany, on May 5, 1818. He was a historian, economist, philosopher, and political theorist. You can say that he is the pioneer of what we know today as communism. While he was living in London after being exiled from his own country, he collaborated with German thinker Friedrich Engels. It is safe to say that Karl Max changed the generation's political and economic belief systems for centuries to come.

Through his works The Communist Manifesto (1848) and Das Kapital (1867–1883), Karl Max changed the face of political, economic, and intellectual systems drastically and disastrously. In his words, the basic idea of his political and economic theory is "From each according to his ability, to each according to his need." According to him, his theory could help eliminate the key channels of profits of the production that the capitalistic owners have and then give the economic and social control into the workers' hands. According to him, this could lead to happy and hard-working individuals doing what they loved, and in return, it would boost the economy. However, his theory didn't prove ideal in many cases that will be discussed later in this book. The other basic idea that Karl Max brought that attracted the masses and still does was "To each according to his need." According to this point, the needy ones are taken care of by the community. Such individuals are provided with the basic stuff and services that are crucial to survival.

## Leninism

Vladimir Ilyich Ulyanov, popularly known as Vladimir Lenin, was born in Simbirsk, Russia, on April 22nd, 1870. This was the Russian Empire era. He was a lawyer and also became the leader of the ruling party of Russia in 1917. He had a hard time in his early life due to his rebellious nature against the undemocratic rule of the king of the Russian Empire, known as Tsar. In short, his brother was executed in 1891, and he was imprisoned for favoring Marxist ideas. I believe this led to Lenin vigorously supporting the political ideologies of Karl Marx. Hence Vladimir Lenin was the Russian version of Karl Marx. He was massively influenced by the political and economic ideologies of Karl Marx.

After going through the works of Karl Marx and Friedrich Engels, Vladimir Lenin published a book known as The Development of Capitalism in Russia in 1899. He was continuously working on Karl Marx's ideologies and officially entered politics by becoming a significant member of the Russian Social Democratic Labor Party. Later, the party divided into two as he was eager to implement socialism without delay, while Julius Martov was in favor of holding on to Marx's theory, which was to implement socialism through capitalism. Hence, Vladimir Lenin's political and economic theory that Marxism inspired is known as Leninism.

Throughout history, the communist leaders brought major historical changes following The Communist Manifesto. In France, the merchant class took control over production, overturning the feudal power structure. Following the footsteps of Karl Marx and Friedrich, many others became the advocates of socialism, bringing the so-called proletarian revolution, then known as socialism, and was later named communism. People thought that the class difference based on property, family structures, and religion would no longer exist in society.

As a result of Lenin's political ideologies and influence on Russia, the Union of Soviet Socialist Republics was established in 1922. It had six communist countries, including Russia, Ukraine, the Transcaucasian Federation, and Belorussia. The influence of Marxism and Leninism went to several other countries as well. It influenced China, giving birth to Maoism or Mao Zedong Thought. Maoism is a variation of Marxism–Leninism and was presented by Mao Zedong as part of his socialist movement. Today, Marxism-Leninism is known to be the fundamental basis of the ideologies of modern communism.

## Communism in Today's Time

Here, I would like to elaborate on the general perceptions about communism. The general perception of communism is that it breaks the chain of inequality that has been consistent throughout history because of the class struggle.

Karl Marx and Friedrich Engels wrote in The Communist Manifesto, "The history of all hitherto existing society is the history of class struggles." Generally, it is perceived that communally-owned means of production and wealth are evenly distributed that is 'to each according to his or her needs and therefore can lead to a more prosperous economy. In contrast, the democratic system is seen as evil for society and opposite to communism. It is because democracy may lead to capitalism and thus form an unequal economic system in which the rich get richer and the poor get poorer. Pro-communists believe that an economy that functions under communist rule will strengthen each individual of the society.

The fancy words and ideas put forward by Karl Marx and Vladimir Lenin gained a lot of attention from the youth of every generation and continue to do so. During my 68 years in America and Brazil, I have observed that the young working middle-class men and women think communism is the key to success and freedom. They believe that the elite is the controller of society and one who benefits from most businesses' profits. The perception of inequality differs from country to country and even person to person. However, I have noticed that the main belief that the masses usually hold regarding inequality is that the elites indulge in wealth, whereas the working class is deprived of its basic rights. They conclude that this happens because of the social class systems and faulty political and economic ideologies. Communism instead of democracy seems a savior and more egalitarian for the working class, labourers, and farmers. Consequently, such people run for the ideologies fed by communist leaders of their country and hence view the collapse of communism as the increment in inequality.

## Issues Concerning Communism

It has been observed that several issues related to economic growth and freedom of the people of the country become apparent with communism as the state ideology. Communism eliminates the free market and therefore works as the key player in stealing the freedom of people to work and grow. Since the market prices are not set by the economic fundamentals of supply and demand and the government sets the prices, this opens an easy pathway for corruption. In this way, the feedback of the demands of the people and seller does not reach the planners, making the price set not updated. The needs of consumers and sellers are not catered to in such an economic system since they do not have a say in what is decided by the communal government. This consequently creates an unbalanced supply and demand system. Moving into this unbalanced system, a black market takes birth to cater to the needs of the citizens, breaking the Marxist rule "to each according to his needs."

From what we discussed above, we can conclude that communism is in direct opposition to the principles of democracy. Therefore, I believe in countries like Brazil, which was saved from becoming a total communist country. It has been a major factor behind the corruption of the previous governments. However, the youth of this generation that belongs to the working class falls readily into the trap of communist leaders and advocates and disregards democracy as the solution of the society.

Many people, including me, believe that democracy is the only solution to eliminate the corruption that arises by implementing the economic and political ideology of communism in the governmental system. I believe I am obliged to convince people for a democratic solution to these issues, including corruption, and bring the practicality of communism into the light. Seeing how the youth is the backbone of our society, the path they are willing to take alarms me— communism. I believe if they are guided properly and enlightened about the past, they will make the right decision, which I strive to do through this book. I will try to elaborate on the issues that communism gives rise to, especially concerning Brazil. Democracy can be a savior to such a society where people are free to choose their leaders and work under the fundamentals of the economic system, and I hope the youth will be able to see this for themselves.

# Chapter 2: Brazil

*"Communism has never come to power in a country that was not disrupted by war or corruption, or both." -**John. Kennedy***

This quote by John. Kennedy always tells me that a country has to have stability. It has to fight poverty and corruption, so it does not fall into the hands of tyrants. But since the beginning of time, the powerful and the rich have always used their power to oppress the weak. They don't oppress just to show how strong they are, but they do it because they are afraid that people one day will stand up to them. A Persian proverb says, "Under the influence of fear, even a coward can show courage." For me, a communist leader is a person who thinks he can do anything he wants. He can take any land he wants. The citizen of that country has no freedom of speech. They can't even complain to anyone. Brazil has seen its share of tyrant leaders, which turned out to be   possible only because the people never tried to fight poverty and corruption. Or maybe they did try, but they were afraid that it would just make things worse.

In the previous chapter, you have learned what communism is and how it has changed our lives. Not only our lives, but it has also changed the political system and the mindset of leaders. As such, communism has been the root cause of all the turmoil that is going on in Brazil.

## Political Problem in Brazil

Brazil has seen some tough times. When it comes to politics, we are one of the worsts, especially when choosing a leader. Brazil's transformation from a country that usually elects moderate and conventional leaders since the beginning of democracy in 1985 to one of the countries that welcomes a candidate who proclaims nostalgia for military rule is a historic political establishment.

A few years ago, I remember that my country was telling the world that it could boost its economy by providing global products. It also hosted both the FIFA World Cup in 2014 and the summer Olympics in 2016. But two recent events have damaged Brazil's economic prospects and people's confidence in its political system. The first problem is China since the factories and shops are closed in Brazil due to COVID-19, people cannot even purchase necessities from their local suppliers.

They have to rely on Chinese products, which are cheaper than the local market. The second problem is Brazil facing a massive corruption scandal, involving the local state oil company Petrobras. It resulted in billions of dollars being plundered from the public treasury, exposing and affecting the entire political class. Over 200 Brazilian politicians, including ex-president Lula, business leaders, and corporations, have all been convicted in the high-level corruption investigation known as Operation Car Wash. This has affected the public trust in our government. According to Gallup, just over 17 % of Brazilians trust our national government, which declined from 51% just a decade ago. During the early days of the investigation, 47 politicians who were charged with corruption or were currently under investigation were defeated in re-election bids. In this frame stepped the 63-year-old congressional backbencher and former paratrooper Bolsonaro, who enjoys a clean record with regard to corruption. He quickly capitalized on public anger. He didn't use traditional ways of campaigning, like massive financing or relying on the structure of traditional parties to appear on the television. He relied on using social media to stay in contact with his supporters.

Since Jair Bolsonaro has taken power, Brazil has seen some new Right Side Parties and some new Left Side Parties. Despite people being afraid of what a Bolsonaro presidency will look like, his rhetorical ways are unlikely to change. He has also made one thing very clear that he does not want Brazil to become another Venezuela. Shortly after winning the first round, he told his supporters, "The good people of Brazil want to get rid of themselves of Socialism; they don't want a Venezuela regime. They want a liberal economy, and they want to defend their family values."

Now that you have read about the political problems being faced by my country, I would like to talk about something I suppose every country faces. That is conspiracy and paranoia around politics. Conspiracy theories around politics have always been spread by those who in some way oppose the current government, whether it's their current policy or how they handle the corrupt officials from the previous government. This is very common in Brazil. When it comes to being paranoid, we are one of the worst countries because we don't trust our government 100%.

# Paranoia and Conspiracy around Brazilian Politics

Ever since Bolsonaro has broken the power of Leftist parties in Brazil, fake news has been spreading around his policies and himself in particular. Like I told you before, this is being done to demoralize the government and break the people's trust in the government. The spread of misinformation, including this fake information being used on the current government, has been under investigation in Brazil since 2019 by a computing Parliamentary Commission created by the National Congress. As stated by the testimonies collected from the investigation, it was identified that a structure linked to the office of the President, nicknamed Office of Hatred, coordinates the spread of misinformation, including defamatory messages against opponents of the President, which were prominent figures from the government.

In the COVID-19 situation, the Commission is presently carrying out a specific investigation into the online profiles that are spreading misinformation related to the pandemic. So far, it has found out an increase in misinformation around three major themes. The first theme is around fake-scientific research about the symptoms, risks, and cures. The second is regarding other countries' prevention and control measures and suggested by the international organizations and their supposedly catastrophic collateral effects. The third theme focuses on attacking or promoting the decision of the government to demoralize the support of social isolation measures and on praising those who support a return to normality like certain government officials and certain people in business.

In addition to this, the Brazilian news agency Lupa, a member of the International Fact-Checking Network, puts together a collection of messages that falsely attribute the positive image to public figures that support the government to enhance its reliability. One of the false messages shows a false donation to fight the COVID-19 by an important business tycoon, who defends the end of isolation. Another one of the false news claims that General Augusto Heleno, head of the Institutional Security Office of the President, was cured by taking the medicine hydroxychloroquine, of which President Bolsonaro is a key advocate. COVID infected Mr. Bolsonaro, and he took the hydroxychloroquine, as I did myself the same. Until last April of 2021, I never got any problems; even when my wife got infected, I got the vaccine Moderna in April because my kids don't allow me to visit them.

To this date, the Commission has not released any sort of evidence to conclude the so-called Office of Hatred or if any member of the Brazilian government is directly involved in coordinating the spread of misinformation about COVID-19. Some part of the government, especially the President himself and his close support of aides, has sustained their denialist stance by conveying misinformation, especially about the symptoms, risk, and cure of COVID-19, and set in motion the risk behavior. Paranoia and conspiracy theories have always been a part of Brazil's history, whether it's about a politician or a situation. There are always people who want to spread fake news. They spread fake news to make life difficult not only for the government but also for the citizens. Now that I have told you all about how miscommunication can cause paranoia and conspiracy theories, let me talk about the history of Brazilian politics.

## History of Brazilian Politics

*"I represent Brazil all over the world. Wherever I go, I have to do my best to not disappoint the Brazilian people. And that I've done." -Pele*

A leader who gets elected should know that the responsibility of a nation is on their shoulder. For me, Pele was a role model because he represents not only himself but also the millions of people living in Brazil. Unfortunately, Brazil has not found even one leader in its long history who represents us as a nation.

Brazil's political evolution from a monarchy to a democracy has not been smooth. After Brazil got independence in the year 1822, unlike its other South-American countries, Brazil adopted constitutional monarchy as its form of government. The newly independent nation retained a slave-based, plantation-based economy and political participation remained very limited. After Dom Pedro II (emperor, 1840-89) acceded to the throne, a two-party system based on the British model, with conservative and liberal parties and recurrent cabinet turnovers, evolved. So what happened was, within this centralized unitary system, the emperor appointed the governors using his entitlement under the moderating power granted by the year 1824 constitution, and legislative elections were unintended. Brazil enjoyed substantial political stability until the year 1880 when the system started to prove incapable of accommodating military demands and pressure to liberate slaves.

Brazil ornamented the constitution of what is now called the Old Republic (1889-1930) on the United States constitution. However, colonialism, a political system based on economic power by large landowners in rural areas, was preserved. Under the new constitution of February 24, 1891, the President, National Congress, state governors and legislatures, and local officials were chosen through direct elections.

After World War I, when Brazil started to undergo rural-urban and agricultural-industrial changes, its political system was unable to cope with the demands of the urban middle classes and mostly the working classes. In the year 1929, the stock market crashed that further exacerbated the evaporative situation. The elites from the states of Rio Grande do Sul, and Minas Gerais staged a pre-emptive revolution and deposed the old regime. As a result of the revolts of the year 1930, Getúlio Dorneles Vargas became president (1930-1945, 1951-1954).

In the year 1930, clashes often used to erupt between the left and the right over different ideologies in major cities of Brazil and often used to turn violent. Vargas often tried to strike a balance between the demands of labor and capital, following Italian leader Benito Mussolini's Carta di Lavoro model of establishment in the 1920s. In 1934, the constitution incorporated this model and thus began the politics of corporatism in Brazil. Vargas was cooperating closely with the military to push for import-substitution industrialization and reduction of military forces under the command of state governments in favor of the Brazilian Armed Forces. In 1937, President Vargas closed down Congress and ruled as a dictator until the year 1945.

The year 1945 to 1965 is known for multi-party democratic politics. Four presidents were elected freely in 1945, 1950, 1955, and 1960. In the early years of the 1960s, the economies grew at a rapid rate, rising inflation, populism, and nationalism, which caused political instability and popular dissatisfaction. The majority of the political parties lost their hegemony, while labor unions gained great political influence over the government of João Goulart, who was the president of Brazil from the year 1961 to the year 1964.

Then in April of 1964, the army seized power and began twenty-one (21) years of rule. Under its model of relative democracy, Congress remained open but was greatly reduced in power. Regular elections were held for congress, state assemblies, and local offices. Nevertheless, presidential, gubernatorial, and some mayoral elections became indirect. The political parties were allowed to operate but with two force realignments. These were the replacement of the old multi-party system with a two-party system in 1965 and a system of moderate pluralism, with six and later five parties in the year 1980. The military regime employed massive repression from the year 1969 to the year 1974.

Following the economic miracle period of the year 1967 to 1974, Brazil entered a stagflation phase concurrent with political liberalization. When the military used to rule the country, Brazil's society became 70% urban. The economy became industrialized, and more manufactured goods than primary goods were being exported. In the same period, about 55% of the population had registered to vote. Foreign policy oscillated between alignment with the United States and pragmatic independence.

A transition of power into a civilian President took place in the year 1985. From the year 1985 to the year 1997, my country was experiencing four distinct political models. It returned to the pre-1964 tradition of political bargaining, clientelism, and economic nationalism under Jose Sarney, who was the President from the year 1985 to 1990. He had an erratic personal style of social nationalism under Itamar Franco, who was the president from the year 1992 to 1994, and a consensus-style social-democratic and neoliberal coalition under Fernando Henrique Cardoso. Fernando was the president of Brazil from the year 1995 to the year 2002.

As you can see, Brazil saw a lot of changes in its political system, yet it did not find any leader who would love to do good for this country. But I hope history can be made under President Bolsonaro, and he could be the leader who will change my country. So, as we now have a leader who is against the left side parties or truly speaking against their ideologies, let me share how we have saved ourselves from communism in the past.

# How Brazil Saved Itself from Communism

My country was seen as a key to the whole of the South-American continent due to its enormously large size and wealth of untouched natural and human resources. The U.S. feared that if Brazil fell to the communists, the rest of Latin America would follow soon after. With the popularity and strength of left-wing and growing communist ideologies through Latin America, Brazil's role grew, and its relationship with the United States became even more important.

It was not only in the interest of the United States that Brazil did not fall into the hands of communism, but local economic elites also had an interest in maintaining a right-wing conservative political climate. Because of President Kubitschek's policy of printing money to cope with foreign debt, rapid inflation meant that Brazilian export volume was decreasing, and the local industries were suffering. The corporatist relationship between the government and the labor unions meant that Goulart's left-leaning government held strategic control over the labor force. The nationalization of important industries, which included oil refining and mineral ore industries, as well as the proposal for radical land reform and redistribution, meant that the power base of the landed economic elite was under attack.

The combined efforts of both the United States and the local economic elites feared being pushed out of power, which did inspire the events that led to the counterrevolution of 1964. The mood of the United States was changing. They were starting to believe that their democratic ideals were rapidly losing ground, and it signaled their desperation for a victory against the persistent forces of communism, especially in Latin America. The signs coming out of Brazil were that the communist forces had worked to create conflict in the country by subverting an anti-illiteracy campaign. This was done so that they could distribute reading aid material that included the Che Guevara guerrilla warfare manual. The communist also wanted to form a Sailors and Marines Association so that they can move the Marxist class war into the army, and it would weaken the military discipline.

Rumors were spreading that the communist force in Brazil was being led by foreign powers, including Chinese and Soviet Union agents. So basically, those standing up to communists were defending their country from a foreign invasion. Those attempting the military coup were not seen as traitors but liberators, thus winning them a high moral ground.

In Brazil, people were supporting the counterrevolution at a similar ideology to the U.S. To promote their ideology in Brazil, U.S. universities were creating business-initiated research groups that were conducting surveys, formulating action plans, and circulating newsletters that closely resembled the progressive technocratic reforms. All of these were occurring throughout the United States in the 1960s. Another thing happening in the U.S. at that time was to establish the power of women so that they can influence public opinion. This attracted many Brazilian women to the ideologies of the United States. All of this combined evoked a sense of awakening within the people, which led to change being cultivated and accepted in Brazil. The progress, although slow, became significant.

You see, it was not only the United States that saved us from communism, but it was also the citizens of Brazil. They were many who bought into the ideas of the Leftist parties. Even I went on to go to vote for President Lula. At first, I thought he was saving the country, but it turned out that he was one of those leaders who only cared what other countries thought of him. He did not care about his own country. He was using the tax payer's money to fund developments in Africa and Cuba and not for his country's citizens who didn't have the necessities. These necessities included medical, housing, and educational reforms and funding. With all of this, it is quite evident that communism was not all it promised. In fact, there was something more behind the ideology of being there together as a nation. It seemed Brazil was everything but communal.

As we come to an end of this chapter, I hope it doesn't change your mind about communism but rather helps you stake your decision, whether you believe in this ideology or not.

# Chapter 3: Bolsonaro

*"Government is instituted for the common good; for the protection, safety, prosperity and happiness of the people; and not for the profit, honor, or private interest of any one man, family, or class of men." -John Adams U.S. President*

The government is supposed to help the common people, those who cannot help themselves. We, the common people, are those who bring the government to power. But sadly, like the U.S President John Adams said, many of the tyrants, those who are in power, use the privileges that we provide them for their profit and honour. They do enough corruption so they can settle their families for life. But others also have families, and those families bought these people to power. Brazil happens to be one of those countries that have seen its leaders misuse their powers, taking things that did not belong to them. But those things that they took belong to the common people.

Every time we elect someone, it is always the same scenario. The leaders that we elect turns out to be corrupt, like ex-President Luiz Inácio Lula da Silva or Dilma Rousseff. We had thought they were good for our country and that they care about it. But it turns out we were wrong, and now we have a new President, a retired military officer, and a conservative. His name is President Jair Messias Bolsonaro. Let's have a look at our President in this chapter and what his regime is like.

# Jair Bolsonaro

Jair Bolsonaro, for his critics, is a dangerous man. He is an advocate for dictatorship, but to his supporters is a leader who is capable of getting Brazil out of political, social, and economic crises. Bolsonaro grew up in Eldorado, a town with a total population of 15,000 people, living in Brazil's Atlantic rain forest. His father used to work as a dentist without a degree, but when more certified dentists arrived, his father shifted to prosthetics. He was the third child in a family that consisted of three sons and three daughters. Bolsonaro used to attend the Preparatory School of the Brazilian Army and graduated from the Agulhas Negras Military Academy in the year 1977.

He was in the army for 17 years, which also included a stint as a paratrooper, and he rose to the rank of captain. Bolsonaro gained some criticism from his superior officer and some fame from his fellow officers and the military families after he wrote an article in the popular magazine Veja. In the article, he wrote negatively about the military pay system. After he left the army in the year 1988, Bolsonaro was elected to a seat in the Rio de Janeiro city council in the year 1989.

Two years later, he won a seat that allowed him to represent Rio de Janeiro in Brazil's Federal Chamber of Deputies. He would hold this seat for seven consecutive terms. Since he was an ex-military man, it was not a surprise when he praised the era of military rule and continuously called for its return from his first term. Bolsonaro was first elected as a member of the Christian Democratic Party, but in the year 1993, he shifted his allegiance to another party, called the Progressive Party. The

Progressive Party went on to form a collation-party with Reform Progressive Party, which became the Brazilian Progressive Party in the year 1995. He again changed the political party allegiance in 2003. This time he joined the Brazilian Labour Party, and in the year 2005, after a brief stint as a member of the Liberal Front, he again returned to the Brazilian Progressive Party, which readopted its name two years ago back to Progressive Party. In the year 2016, he joined the Social Christian Party.

Well, his fortune change when Brazil's political culture went downward in the second decade of the 21st century, and Brazil's economy also went along for the ride. At the beginning of the second presidential term of Dilma Rousseff, who was from the "Workers Party," the country went deeper into a recession that had begun in the year 2014, which according to a lot of observers, was Brazil's worst economic crisis since the turn of the 20th century. During this time, there was another thing developing in Brazil, the biggest political scandal in Brazilian history- the Petrobras scandal.

The Petrobras scandal inundate the majority of Brazil's mainstream politicians with allegations of corruption. Even Rousseff was impeached and removed from office because of financial accounting improprieties. Even her successor, Michel Temer, was targeted with an accusation of wrongdoing which saw his public approval rating dropping to single digits. During this time, violence and crime in Brazil went out of control.

As the campaign for the 2018 Brazilian Presidential election began in earnest, Luiz Inácio Lula da Silva, who is mostly known as Lula, became the political mentor of the ex-president Rousseff. Now, Lula was widely popular when he was the president from 2003 to 2011 and became the clear front-runner. Even though at that time he was involved in the Petrobras scandal, which led to his conviction on charges of corruption and money laundering in July 2017 that was upheld in a January 2018 ruling, he was sent to prison for 12 or more years, in April 2018. While Lula continuously tried to seek that he be allowed to run for presidential elections even though he was convicted, Bolsonaro, who at that time was a candidate of the insignificant Social Liberal Party, started a populist campaign with which he sought to take advantage of Brazilians' widespread distrust of the political establishment amid the corruption scandal.

Because Bolsonaro was an outsider, a person who was new in politics quickly took advantage by calling himself an anti-establishment insurgent candidate with little concern for traditional political ways. Bolsonaro soon won the support from the country's considerable Evangelical Christian population because he is steadfast in opposition to abortion and his promise to bring in new policies in law-and-order so that crime and violence in Brazil could be reduced.

In early August, the Workers Party chose Lula to be its candidate. But after the Superior Electoral Court ruled on August 31 that Lula was "ineligible" to run for the presidency, on September 11th, Lula withdrew from the election and supported his running mate, Fernando Haddad. Fernando was the former mayor of Sao Paulo. As soon as Lula departed from the race, Bolsonaro became the clear favorite in the contest.

During the first round of voting on October 7, he was far ahead of the rest of the 13-candidates, capturing 46% of the vote but falling short of the 50 % margin that was required to prevent the runoff. So the stage was set for a head-to-head battle on October 28 with Haddad, who finished the first round with 29 % of the votes. He could not take enough votes in the runoff, as Bolsonaro swept to a commanding victory in the runoff, taking more than 55% of the vote to become Brazil's president-elect.

Now Bolsonaro was elected president, and he did try to change things for the better, but like every leader, he too has flaws. No leader can come and tell you that he won't make mistakes. Those in power will always be a threat to the citizen of a country, or they could also be a threat to themselves. Sometimes when someone gets too much power, they start losing control. Now I am not saying that Bolsonaro will also be the same, but I will tell you how some of his policies can be a threat to Brazil.

## Threats Toward Brazil

In the past, Bolsonaro supported the country's dictatorship era, which he called the "golden era" of Brazil. It was a time of terror for most of Brazil, where the tyrants were running the country like their playground. Many people disappeared during that time. This does not mean that he is not trying to change Brazil for the better. Had he not been a good leader, then many Brazilian elite businessmen would not have supported him. When President Lula of the Workers Party was elected in 2002, the prospect of a left-wing government shook Brazil's business-class elitists and its international supporters. Many businessmen initially withdrew their support from the Brazilian economy because they were reluctant to invest, leading the stock market to collapse. This followed with the Brazilian currency collapsing and the costs of government borrowing escalating. As a result, Lula was forced to promise the business increased macroeconomic stability to control inflation and seek fiscal equilibrium.

This formed a surprising alliance between Lula's left-wing government and the country's most powerful businessmen association. Lula's social and economic agenda was dubbed "New Developmentalism." It aimed to support the development of Brazilian multinationals, which provided low-interest loans from the State Bank (BNDES). Many experts called this economic policy the "FIESP agenda" (after the most powerful business association, the Federation of Industries of São Paulo). It showed how close the ties were between the big business and the Workers Party government for most of the 2000s. Despite Lula's government having such close ties with the business community, he also launched redistribution policies, such as the "bolsa familia," which financially rewarded the poor families, granted they promised to keep their children in school and health programs. This did have some benefits, such as many businesses expanding globally. Now all of this sounds too good to be true, right, but that is how the left-wing parties made us all feel. Although, things were going to go down for the Workers Party. This was because the relationship between the left-wing government and the big business started to turn sour. From the year 2012 onwards, the Workers Party government, was now under Rousseff. It was less favorable in the international business communities due to the declining global commodity prices, damaging Brazilian exports. This led to a growing gap in Brazil between state revenue and expenditure, followed by high levels of borrowing and the threat by the government to increase the tax.

There was also the case of the poor quality of public services and infrastructure projects, which included the 2012 football World Cup and 2016 Olympics. Apart from these, there was growing evidence of large-scale corruption among Brazilian politicians from all parties, which led to massive street protests in June 2013. President Bolsonaro used social media to stoke up fears about urban violence, the destruction of "traditional" moral values and the family, and the prevalent corruption of the Brazilian establishment.

During his 27 years in Congress, President Bolsonaro was supported by protectionism and powerful businessmen communities. He has appointed Chicago-trained Paulo Guedes as his economic adviser in a direct attempt to reassure big business. President Bolsonaro had also begun to expose more pro-market views. It is not a surprise that the business elite, including FIESP's President, Paulo Skaf, have supported Bolsonaro because they believe he could deliver their economic agenda. On the other hand, Brazil today faces a perfect storm of a healthcare disaster, economic collapse, and social implosion. Along with these, Brazil has the most militarized government globally, which Jair Bolsonaro runs, but many people forget that Bolsonaro was not the one who created these problems. These problems were created by those who came before him, the Left-Wing parties. So, what happened to him was amid the growing coronavirus infection and deaths, a judge of the Brazilian Supreme Court dropped a bombshell by saying that the army was associating itself with a "genocide."

In the last couple of months, the ministry is being run by General Eduardo Pazuello, a serving officer with no healthcare experience. Since Bolsonaro fired Luis Mandetta, who was a popular health minister and his successor, in a matter of 30 days, Bolsonaro has shown no signs of appointing a full-time minister. Now, you must understand something, Bolsonaro is an ex-military guy. Thus, it is going to take him time to set things right for Brazil.

In January 2019, when Bolsonaro took power, he appointed many retired and currently serving Generals to his Cabinet. Out of the 23 ministers in the federal government, ten are from the armed forces. According to a report from the Federal Audit Bureau, some 6,157 military personnel, whether in active service or retired, hold a civilian position in the government. There is some 1,249 military personal in the health ministry alone. The data only came out when another Supreme Court judge warned of the "risk of militarisation" of government. Brazil's civil society and the media have been raising questions about whether Bolsonaro will militarise the government or not. Brazil's top newspaper, Folha de Sao Paulo revealed that active-duty military personnel in government departments grew by 33% since Bolsonaro came to power.

From the 1990s until 2016, the report indicated that the military personnel only served in the Ministry of Defence and Security Offices. But since Bolsonaro came to power, they are holding more important positions across the departments, ranging from education to health and culture. Since he has taken power, he has often used the military name to warn the country's opposition and institutions like the Congress and Supreme Court. He has also openly participated in far-right rallies that demand "military intervention." Now what he faces might be the biggest crisis of his term; choosing General Pazuello to lead Brazil's response to coronavirus. He also appointed another 24 persons with a military background in key positions in the Ministry of Health. He ordered the army to quickly mass-produce anti-malarial drugs, chloroquine, and hydroxychloroquine – for public distribution.

With so many people dying in Brazil due to the COVID-19 pandemic, now the citizens of my country are not even allowed to enter Uruguay and Paraguay. Bolsonaro had a conversation with Justice Mendes. During this conversation, it has emerged that Justice Mendes warned him about the possibility of pandemic negligence being taken to the International Criminal Court at The Hague. The judge continuously told Bolsonaro that he had heard about this possibility in some conversation in Europe during their conversation. This was coming from a top judge; "genocide" became a front-page headline in Brazil. Although, for the rest of the world, the word has been in discussion for some time. Global Justice activist Monique Cruz denounced Brazil at the UN Human Rights Council, "Brazilian prisons are a fundamental part of the State's genocidal project."

She also condemned the government for not releasing the prisoners as the virus spread in its overcrowded jails.

Furthermore, newspapers have shared that a group of Brazilian parliamentarians sent a letter to the WHO director-general in April. In those articles, these parliamentarians accused the President of "flirting with the risk of genocide." Also, in recent months, several human rights groups have filed a complaint at the ICC against Bolsonaro for causing a "risk of genocide" of indigenous people in the Amazon region. This, too, puts the Bolsonaro – and Brazilian military – in a tight spot. Everyone is trying to discredit Bolsonaro; what they want is to regain power and overthrow the President.

*"The accomplice to the crime of corruption is frequently our own indifference." -Bess Myerson*

People commit crimes and corruption because they think this will lead their families to a better life and a brighter future. What they don't realize is that by committing a crime, they are destroying not only their soul but also the soul of the country, which they belong to. When you commit corruption, the entire foundation collapses as you are stealing from your brothers and sisters. The Left-Wing did the same. They stole from us for years. Corruption is not new to Brazil. It has been going on for decades. Let me tell you some of the renowned cases of corruption that sprung to notice.

# Crime and Corruption in Brazil

When we talk about crime and corruption in Brazil, the first thing that comes to my mind is Operation Car Wash. It all started with the arrest of an oil executive by the name of Nestor Cervero. He was arrested on charges of corruption. It was a turning point that shook Brazil to its core because it was the breakthrough that the investigators were looking for in the Car Wash corruption investigation. The case that led toward the arrest of a major oil executive was named Lava Jato by the press. The press and the public were all over the case because the case discovered a huge level of corruption, which the media describe as the biggest corruption investigation in the history of Brazil. But it did not just involve Brazil. It had its root globally as the investigation found out that many countries and foreign firms were involved.

There was also the case of the illegal payment of more than five billion dollars to many of the big company executives and members of the political establishment. The investigation led to many business people going to jail and collapsing the sitting Brazilian government. It did collapse not only the sitting government but also the government that was to follow after. Ex-president Rousseff was impeached, and ex-president Michel Temer faced a hard time due to this corruption scandal. Though, corruption is not the only problem that Brazil faces. Brazil also witnesses the world's most violent crimes. Brazil is Latin America's largest economy, but it faces a new era of violence and crime, as its pacification strategies in response to crimes in the major cities have become a thing of the past.

President Jair Bolsonaro has promised drastic measures that will shift the country's security situation. One of them is to ease the legal requirements for purchasing and carrying firearms and softening sanctions for the act of abuse, which is committed by state agents. Until now, Brazil has had one of the highest rates of police brutality on the continent. Brazil is also the home of two of the largest criminal gangs in South America. They are called the First Command and the Red Command. They are mostly involved in the international trade of drugs, arms dealing, and contraband smuggling. They also have violent control over Brazilian prisons. That means these two gangs have a major influence over the Brazilian government.

These are not the only gangs in Brazil, the more dangerous than these two are the Militias, who are made up of current and former police officers. Their business relies on extortion and extrajudicial killings. These gangs would not even have existed if Brazil was not a prime location for drugs that are smuggled to Europe. Not only that, but many Brazilians also take drugs. This has made life difficult not only for the law enforcement agencies but also the ordinary citizens. There have been many law and order policies in Brazil, yet nothing triumphs over crime yet. Even this does not stop President Bolsonaro from implementing a bill that will tackle violent crimes in the country.

## Law and Order

The current Brazilian President, Jair Bolsonaro, has attempted to stop the crime rate in Brazil by signing many policies that should stop the flow of some of the violent crimes in Brazil. The current administration has also responded by saying that the policies that are implemented by the current president will help to reduce crime throughout Brazil. Bolsonaro did promise when he was campaigning for the elections that his first policy when he assumes office would reduce the crime rate.

Brazil has witnessed at least 1,060,000 murder cases since 2000. While the murder rate has skyrocketed over the thirty (30) years, the Brazilian government has not seriously tried to tackle this problem on the national level. Even Brazil Minister of Justice and Public Security, Sergio Moro, has given clear signals that reducing violent crime is a key agenda for him and President Bolsonaro's government.

While the previous governments did attempt to try to stop the flow of violent crime that is rocking Brazilian society in the year 2017, these initiatives appeared not to be working or did not have a lasting impact. While Brazil has not done anything to tackle this situation, some states are trying to tackle the problem on their own. While not all the plans have worked so far, they did show signs of reducing the crime rate throughout these states. The state that has come up with one of the most effective plans to reduce the crime rate in Sao Paulo started to make plans in the 1990s. The state witnessed a huge drop in the crime rate, especially violent crime, with the murder rate reducing from 33.1 per 100,000 in 2001 to 6.4 per 100,000 in 2018. The Metropolitan area of Sao Paulo saw even more reduction in the crime rate, dropping from 49.2 per 100,000 in

2001 to just over 5.5 per 100,000 as per the current year. It makes Sau Paulo one of the safest cities in Brazil.

Many experts believe that the current status of the decline in the crime rate is because Brazil is facing a reduction in its youth population. The employment rate is much higher, meaning more people in Brazil have jobs. One of the key factors is that more police reforms are being done in a country that has a history of police brutality. The policies that are changing are having a major impact on the Brazilian criminal world. Some of these changes are crime mapping, improvement in the training of the police force, and the strengthening of ties between the civil and the military police. There is also the case that some of the major criminal organizations in Brazil, like the Primeiro Commando de Capital have created a pax mafiosa, which have hugely contributed to the reduction of crimes in the country.

## The Economy of Brazil

I heard in a newspaper that recently, the Brazilian committee for Monetary Policy that is mostly known as COPOM, had a meeting in which they discussed the current economic environment, not only of Brazil but also the world. The meeting had one common agenda, and that was to maintain the current interest rate. The committee decided to keep Brazil Taxa Selic at two percent per annum. Although this might not be important to many people, it does tell the Brazilian people and the people from around the world about the recovery of the economy of the biggest economy in South America.

The Brazilian State Bank is not like its counterparts from around the world like U.S. Federal Reserves. Brazil State Bank has just one goal, and that is to keep the inflation level down. COPOM is the federal committee chosen by the government to adjust the interest rate. In Brazil, to identify the interest rate and the interest rate that guides the local market is called the Taxa Selic. The committee's job is to decrease or increase the Taxa Selic so that it can make the Brazilian currency cheap or expensive. As a result of the interest rate dropping, many consumers become reluctant to spend or save their money which affects inflation directly. Because if the people of Brazil do not spend their money, it means the prices cannot increase, which will eventually increase the demand to increase the prices of the goods being sold in Brazil.

In the past two decades, Brazil had a very high Taxa Selic. Usually, when you see a double-digit interest rate, it means the economy is growing very slowly as big business people and enterprises refuse to borrow money from the banks. Many countries rely on credit lines and other forms of borrowing, such as debt issuing. These are important for the economic growth of a country. Brazil's recent GDP is very weak compared to other countries in South America. According to experts, the facilitation of capital acquisition by many enterprises will bring about more production, a low level of unemployment, and the development of industries.

For the past nine meetings, COPOM is cutting the interest rates. It decided to maintain the current Taxa Selic, which showed it did not believe that the Brazilian economy required an extra push. Instead, it has decided to play cautiously because it fears the possibility of inflation. So for me, this decision is a good sign from the central bank of the biggest economy of South America, which also signals positive signs that the Brazilian economy is toward recovery.

The current Brazilian president Bolsonaro wants to introduce a new welfare program Renda Cidada, which will be introduced by next year and is going to replace the existing emergency off-budget aid that was introduced this year. The idea of the government is to merge it with the current Bolsa Familia, a program that will cost around 35 billion reais per year. But the problem is the Brazilian government has not made clear how it intends to fund the project without it breaking the government's spending cap fiscal rule, which will also limit the growth in public expenditure to the current annual rate of inflation.

Another bill Pension Reform was passed in October 2019. It was a major step because it changed the Brazilian constitution. Because of the high cost of the bill, which is a major concern for Brazil's huge fiscal deficit, the situation was made worse with the 2016 slow economic growth and the increasing number of Brazil's aging population. According to the data collected by the Organization for Economic Cooperation and Development, the government deficit-to-GDP ratio stood at 7.8 percent in 2017 and 7.1 percent in 2018. If these numbers continue, it will save Brazil 195 billion dollars in the next ten years.

To consider it all, economy, corruption, and crime, these factors aren't solely responsible, nor do they entirely contribute to the current situation faced by Brazil. There is also a far dangerous thing, and that is the controversy surrounding Brazilian politics. The government is being led by the Economy Minster Guedes, who is involved in economic fronts, including privatization and selling more than 23-billion-dollar state assets in 2019. It will ease the monetary policy with some of the lowest interest rates in Brazil's recent history and implement deregulation measures.

Even though Brazil's economy was weak in the first quarter of 2019, it showed signs of a stronger expansion in the second quarter of the same year. So the real GDP growth was more likely going to be disappointing 1.0 percent in the year 2019, but the forecast did show a positive sign for the year 2020, until the COVID-19 global crisis.

## Controversial Lines

As the corruption charges affected both sides of the political field, a cut-down of some of the more controversial thoroughness proposals that were implemented by the ex-president Temer administration still affect the Brazilian people. On March 15, 2017, some 1,500 activists took part in a massive protest that occupied the streets outside the Ministry of Finance in Brasilia. The main agenda of the protest was to oppose the government proposal to restructure Brazil's massive social security program. This led to a huge day of debating against labor reforms and the proposed social security changes that were organized by social movements and trade union leaders, which attracted up to a million people to the street across Brazil.

This protest showed the ongoing effort by left-wing forces to block the neoliberal economic and social policies of the government of ex-president Michel Temer, who came into power in 2016 after the impeachment of President Dilma Rousseff. Two weeks later, on March 26, 2017, thousands of right-wing political opponents of the former Rousseff government took part in a protest that rocked Brazil.

It was to show their support of the investigation about the alleged corruption done by the Workers Party ex-president Lula and ex-president Dilma Rousseff. Although the turnout was smaller than the massive protest that the right-wing parties organized in 2015 and 2016, Brazil remains politically polarized with conservative politicians that still hold the upper hand.

The right-wing wave that was getting popular in Brazil was part of an international trend, yet it took a particularly serious national toll as Brazil's economy and political institutions were being damaged significantly reputation-wise over the past few years. After the Party of the Brazilian Democratic Movement's wrangling of power from the Workers Party, it was very difficult for the Temer's government to establish or maintain the legal rights of their government. Plus, Temer has proposed several bills that were unpopular in front of the general public. He wanted those bills to pass so that he could carry out a series of controversial structural reforms. His approval rating throughout his time was in single digits.

Additionally, the ongoing conflict among executives, legislatures, the judicial branches, and the routine arrest of prominent business people and political figures charged with corruption happening in the middle of an ongoing economic crisis had dampened the optimistic predictions being made in recent years that Brazil was becoming the twenty-first-century world power.

The economy was already showing signs of slowing down during the 2014 presidential elections, which gave Rousseff a narrow win over Aécio Neves, her central-right opponent. But then, the 2016 impeachment case of the former revolutionary on the grounds of failing to comply with the budgetary regulation did deepen Brazil's crisis even more. There was a leaked telephone conversation among the Brazilian Democratic Movement party members, which revealed that the party leaders were planning to oust Rousseff so that they could block the ongoing corruption investigation into their financial handlings. Somehow, Temer was able to convince the majority of the Congress that, as President, he would both fix Brazil's economy and political problems. At the same time, he also promised to stop government corruption. However, he did not fulfill any of his promises. Data was released in 2016 that showed since 2014, the Gross Domestic Product dropped 7.2% in the absolute term and 9.1% per capita. Brazil also plunged into the worst recession in its history during the Temer term. However, some experts believe that Brazil's economy will recover by the year 2024.

Temer made many promises, but his initiatives made things even worse. They extended Brazil's economic crisis. His conservative fiscal measures targeted many of the social guarantees that were outlined in the year 1988, according to the

Federal Constitution. Among his most controversial actions, the Constitutional Amendment 55 that he made comes at the top. It froze all federal government expenditures for the next twenty (20) years. It only allowed adjustments that were based on inflation. It means health and education, which were already two of the underfunded areas that required investment, were going to suffer even more in the years to come.

What can help all of this? What can help Brazil overcome corruption properly without having to sacrifice to the development of the country? I believe alternatives such as selecting the right form of government can improve the political and economic situation of our country.

## The Alternative

The alternative to all of Brazil's problems for me is our current president, Jair Bolsonaro. He is strong opposition to the left-wing politicians, who have ruined Brazil and sent it into abysses. He also supports land reforms, which are essential to the growth and infrastructure of Brazil. In an interview he gave to a journalist, Bolsonaro said that his views are similar to the centrist right-wing United States citizens.

It is known how the United States views gun ownership, abortion, gender-based politics, and trade. Its approach seems to be fair and just. During election campaigns, Bolsonaro promised that he intended to reverse some disarmament laws and improve public security and trade ties with the United States, which were broken during ex-president Lula and Rousseff's government.

During the 2018 presidential campaign, President Bolsonaro said he would make a considerable change to Brazil's foreign relations. He said that Brazil's foreign relations should be in service to the value that was always associated with the Brazilian people. He also said that Brazil should stop supporting dictators and stop attacking democracies.

In 2018, Bolsonaro again confirmed his commitment by making foreign trips to the United States, Israel, Japan, South Korea, and Taiwan. When he returned, he told the press that during the trip, he realized Brazil would soon be following in the footsteps of one of these countries. It was crucial for Brazil's betterment. He stated how he would love to follow in the footsteps of the good people who care about their country.

Bolsonaro also showed his distrust toward China. Throughout his campaigns, he claimed that China intends to buy entire Brazil, even though Brazil recorded a US$20 billion trade with China in the year 2018, not to mention China is the 13th largest source of direct foreign investment into Brazil. He did mention that he would do business with the Chinese, but he would prefer other countries that had no hidden ideologies or agenda behind them. His stance on China changed when he took office, adding that he would stay out of the ongoing China-U.S. trade war.

The current political situation that is grappling Brazil, both economically and politically, can be credited to the past leaders of Brazil, like ex-president Lula, ex-president Rousseff, and ex-president Temer. They all did not care about Brazil but themselves. Alternatively, Bolsonaro also has his faults, but he has made his agenda clear. He is looking out for Brazil. For him, Brazil comes first, and he wants to defeat the ideology of corruption. All of this, however, happens to be my perception that I wish to share with you. I hope as we reflect on the corruption that took place, we can trace it to the root cause and avoid making the same mistake twice.

# Chapter 4: The Leftists in Brazil

*"The Labor Party believes in turning workers against owners; we believe in turning workers into owners."* — *Margaret Thatcher*

The Labor party of Brazil thought that they were altering the country by bringing in a revolution like the communist government of Fidel Castro did in Cuba. No, they were not changing Brazil. They were just making people oblivious to their fake ideologies. Even after they lost their government, they tried to spread their ideologies to destabilize the current government of President Jair Bolsonaro. As Margaret Thatcher said, the Labor Party believes in turning the workers against their owners. Well, for me, she was truly the Iron Lady because she saw right through what the Labor Party's actual ideologies were.

In hopes of shedding some light on the ideologies rising through Brazil, I will discuss the history of the Workers Party and the numerous Leftist Parties of Brazil in this chapter, how they spread their corrupt ways to the Brazilian people, and how they eventually destroyed my beloved country of Brazil.

## Workers Party of Brazil, the Left-Wing Party

One of the major events that occurred in Brazilian politics was when the Workers Party of Brazil came into power. It all began with Ex-President Lula coming into power in 2002. It started a period in which the Workers Party, also known as PT, saw its power increasing year by year. The increase in their influence saw the Lula protégée Ex-President Rousseff coming into power in 2011. She stayed in power until her impeachment in 2016. The Party was first established by a group of militants who were against Brazil's military establishment that saw them as a tyrant destroying the country. It was made up of people from the trade union, left-wing university professors, celebrities, and people from the Catholic Church. The party was established in 1980 in Sao Paulo.

The Workers Party was established under the socialist ideology. It was formed after the 1964 coup by Getulio Vargas. Many union leaders saw their organization members being reduced due to the military interfering in how it chooses its leadership. Since the Labor Party was formed, its leaders were chosen by the Ministry of Labor, and since the government was terrorizing the local union to control it, the Labor Party led a movement of local strikes. These local strikes were led by Lula, which revolutionized the entire Labor Party. Its purpose was that the local federal government did not get involved in the matters of the union.

But the survival of the Workers Party was getting affected by the influence of the trade union, which was being led by left-wing parties. Their ideologies were different than the Workers Party. So the Workers Party came up with a different approach, influenced by leaders with an anti-Stalin ideology. These ideologies helped the Workers Party form themselves on the basis of a similar concept of union movements that were ongoing in Poland.

Since 1988, the Workers Party has been increasing its influence all over Brazil. It did so by winning the local elections in Sao Paulo, Fortaleza, Belo Horizonte, Porto Alegre, and Goiania. Not only in the biggest cities of Brazil, but they were also winning the elections in some of the major states, the Rio Grande do Sul, Espirito Santo, and Federal District. This winning momentum was due to its leader Lula who became the leader of the party after Luiz Gushiken, who was the leader of the party from December 11, 1988, to July 15, 1990.

In the elections of 1989, even though Lula had the support of the central parties' candidates and the left-wing party's candidates, he lost to Fernando Collor in the second round by a close margin. His loss was due to Fernando being supported by the media. But it did give the Workers Party the platform that showed the Brazilian people the growing influence it was having on the political establishment in the years to come.

In the elections of 1994, Lula was leading in the polls and was expected to win the general election. But because Fernando had the support of the central party, which supported Lula in the previous election, the right-wing party won the election in the first round. This was since Fernando was in power. He introduced a financial bill that saw a new currency being introduced. This, in return, saw the end to inflation that provided the Brazilian economy with a boost to its economy. The elections saw the Brazilian Workers Party gaining some momentum since their two candidates were elected governors for two states. But the result was the same in the elections of 1998, which again saw Fernando being elected as the President of Brazil. Due to the economic crisis in Asia in the year 1997, it was affecting the economy of Brazil, which was making the second term of Ex-President Fernando difficult. Ever since he was re-elected in the 1998 general elections, the Brazilian people saw a currency crisis. The crisis affected the overall economy, and the employment rate dropped to its lowest point. The results were reflected in Lula gaining influence among the Brazilian people, which also attracted the attention of investors, both from other countries and within Brazil. These investors thought that if Lula won the 2002 elections, it would destroy the Brazilian economy even more because he was a candidate of the Workers Party.

It was known that the Worker Party's ideology openly supported a transfer of the Brazilian economy to a socialist economy. So what Lula did, as he promised the Brazilian people that if he is elected the President of Brazil, he will not change the economic policies of Brazil. In the end, the promise he made saw the Workers Party feeling betrayed by his stance because they did want a change in the Brazil policies.

But after three attempts, Lula did win the general elections in 2002. He won it by a big margin of 61.3%, which at that time was the second-best performance in a general election in the world after the Ronald Regan elections in 1984. But Lula did not win the elections easily, since, in the first round, he did not get the required vote that would have declared his victory. He had to win the elections in the second round. This began his presidential career, which saw him stay in power until the general elections of 2010, after which his protégée Ex-President

Rousseff came into power until Rousseff's impeachment in the year 2016, due to the allegations of corruption. Now the impeachment of Rousseff led to a downfall of the Workers Party, in which it did not only see them lose their power and influence but also saw their leaders going to jail due to the corruption scandal. The scandal was called Operation Car Wash. But since the election victory of Lula, the Brazilian Leftist Parties did see their influence spreading throughout the country.

## Socialist Movement in Brazil

To look at the Socialist Movement that is influencing the Brazilian establishment, we have to go back in history to the year 1892, when the first Socialist Congress was established in Rio de Janeiro. During the same year, another Socialist Congress was created that was split from the Socialist Congress, which was established before. In the same year, Brazil saw the establishment of the Socialist Party of Brazil in Rio de Janeiro. This was the start of a movement that was bound to change the dimension of Brazilian politics for years to come.

But it was not until the year 1902 when Brazil saw the foundation of a major Socialist Party that was created by a migrant from Italy. The migrant was known as Alcibiades Bertollotti, who was also the founder of a newspaper that supported the Italian Socialist Party. In the same year, the Socialist Collective Party was formed in the State of Rio de Janeiro, whose leader was Vincente de Souza. He was a teacher. Its co-leader was Gustavo Lacerda, who was a journalist. In

1906, Brazil saw another socialist party found by the name of the Independent Workers Party. The Socialist movement saw its influence increase during World War I but remained mostly underground. The socialists were able to spread their influence from the shadows. In 1919, another Socialist Party was formed by the name of the Socialist League. The party members started spreading their ideologies throughout Brazil by publishing them in newspapers in 1921. In the year 1925, another socialist party was formed by the name of the Brazilian Socialist Party, whose leader was Evaristo de Morais.

After the 1964 Coup, the numerous socialist parties of Brazil saw their influence being diminished because of the military government silencing them because the governments found the Socialist ideologies a threat to their regime. So the Socialist parties formed guerilla groups that were against the military government, but in fact, it was a way for them to spread their influence and start a revolution throughout Brazil as Fidel Castro did in Cuba.

In 1984, the Landless Workers Movement was established because they thought the military administration was not doing their jobs in their land reform policies. This saw the growth of influence of the Socialist Party that started to influence the mindset of the Brazilian people for years to come.

It suffices to say that from the year 2002, since Lula came into power, to 2016, when Rousseff was impeached, Brazil's socialist movement saw its influence increasing. Their power increased to the point that it became a part of life for the Brazilian people to a time when their ideologies started diminishing rapidly since the Workers Party came under scrutiny for the numerous corruption they did in the name of the Brazilian people.

In the elections of 1989, the Brazilian Workers Party allied with numerous other Leftist parties and made Lula, their candidate. Despite the elite-class of Brazil fearing that if the Workers Party came into power, they would try to change the land reform policies that could have made them lose their lands, Lula did promise them that he would not apply any socialist policy to his rule, but he did lose the election because the people did not trust him.

The reason behind the people not trusting Lula was simple. They did not see him doing anything constructive. When you watch your country being destroyed by the establishment you pick, your view about them will change in a negative way. The Workers Party, when first elected, promised to be a government that represented the Brazilian people. But the years of corruption made people look at their ideologies in a different light. As such, the Brazilian people viewed the leftist parties and the right-wing parties differently.

## Opinion on the Left and Right Wings

Even though ex-president Rousseff was impeached, followed by ex-president Michel Temer being arrested in 2019, the Workers Party's popularity remained strong among its supporter. The supporters of the Workers Party called out the corruption investigation. They called it a witch hunt to destabilize the Workers Party. But the opinion of the Brazilian people is different because they did elect Jair Bolsonaro as their president. After all, they were tired of the corruption and tyranny that the previous administrations of the leftist ideologies were doing.

Even though Bolsonaro is a far-right politician and some of his policies may not be popular among the Brazilian people, yet ever since he took power, he has had strong support from the businessmen of Brazil. This is mainly due to his economic policies, thanks to the Brazilian economy minister Paulo Guedes. The minister supports the idea of the Central Bank of Brazil working independently. He also supports that the companies owned by the federal government should be made private. Additionally, he wants to introduce a capitalization system that will benefit social security.

The Social Security policy was the downfall for the previous administration as it failed to get it to be passed by the Brazilian Parliament. But the administration of President Jair Bolsonaro gains a major victory after the Brazilian Parliament passed their Pension Reform bill, which gave the Brazilian economy the boost that it was looking for. Even Jair Bolsonaro's policy will benefit the local businessmen since it allows them to directly negotiate trade deals with different companies from around the world.

Now when it comes to the rule of the Workers Party, especially ex-president Lula, there are mixed opinions against him. Some view him as a person who frees the country from an elite class and gives everyone equality, and some view him as just another socialist leader who just wants to spread his party's ideologies by making shady alliances. On the other hand, Jair Bolsonaro had been clear about his policies and allegiances to the Brazilian people.

This made him popular among the people, especially during the current COVID-19 crisis that has shaken the world. Despite him not taking the disease drastically initially, which dropped his approval rating shockingly low, recently, his administration has come up with a policy in which they are giving away cash to the families who have no source of income due to the current pandemic. His supporters were the rich and powerful. However, because of his latest policies, he can be seen gaining supporters from the poor communities as well. His approval rating has also increased, which comes as a surprise to himself and all the critics who deemed his government to fail due to his policies.

When the world was going into lockdown, Bolsonaro had urged that the Brazilian government should remain open. He said the people without any luxuries or income wouldn't be able to survive a lockdown, which gained him a lot of supporters from the lower-income groups. Alternatively, based on a political expert's analysis, he stopped scolding the different government departments, stopped sacking people, and started to form strong alliances with parties. As a result, his changed behavior earned him a better approval rating from the people. And why shouldn't he? He is implementing changes that cater to the need of Brazilians.

Even the people from the poorest parts of the country, who once supported the Lula's Worker Party, such as a city name Guaribas, started to support Jair Bolsonaro. They did so because of his recent decision about not closing down the Brazilian economy. The local hotel owners are being benefited by the current administration as well. They are building roads where there was only dirt. Whether it is a direct or indirect move, the people are seeing changes from the current administration. Alas! There is a constraint to his ruling. The Brazilian government cannot keep supporting the Brazilian people, inching Jair Bolsonaro closer to an impeachment chance. What makes this possible is his continuous support to the poor communities. Some politicians believe he may bankrupt the Brazilian economy by giving to the poor a little too much, but not me, I thrust him.

Now, this is the problem where much of Brazilian changed its views about politicians or their ideologies. Jair Bolsonaro is trying to help the people because he knows that the years of corruption and mishandling of certain policies have crippled the Brazilian economy. But because the economy is weak, he cannot even help the poor communities out as he wishes. While he faces severe challenges, it does not imply that he is not trying to change the country. He is making policies that will save the country from the corruption of the leftist parties, having a strong battle against the legislation trying to pass his plans, which is barred time and time again.

## How Is the Brazilian Left-Wing under Threat from Brazil's Recent Shift to Right-Wing Politics?

During his election campaigns, President Bolsonaro has promised his supporters that he will cleanse the country of the left-wing parties. He said this because years of corruption done by the leftist parties had led the Brazilian economy into ruins. The economic crash resulted in a surge in crimes in many parts of the country. Many people are without a source of basic income.

While the economy is a major factor in imposing that the leftist is under threat from Jair Bolsonaro's right-wing government, it is the approach that Left-Wing Lula and Right-Wing Jair Bolsonaro are competing to win the support of the people. It was essential here that the people change their ideologies from that in 2002. Where people first supported the left-wing policies, by the year 2018, they were supporting far-right ideologies.

Lula used policies that were already in use by the former administration, which did ease the inequality rate and improve the economy. Jobs were created in working-class communities. His policy also resulted in one of the largest welfare programs in the world, which made him one of the popular presidents of Brazilian history. But it was also due to these policies that he was accused of mass corruption and brought the Brazilian economy to a total collapse.

On the other hand, the right-wing party took advantage. Bolsonaro took advantage of the Brazilian people's anger from the left-wing parties, especially the Workers Party. He made the Right-Wings ideologies about the people, resulting in them shifting their allegiances toward Jair Bolsonaro.

When ex-president Lula was in office, he had a closer relationship with Cuba, Venezuela, and a shaky relationship with the U.S. He made international headlines when he rejected farm subsidies. Because of this, he walked out of the World Trade Organization talks in 2003, damaging Brazil's foreign relationship quite badly. Now when the Workers Party was in power, it was more lenient to countries like China that were silently taking over Brazil's economy.

Now that Jair Bolsonaro has come into power, he has promised that he will not let China take over Brazil. This will hamper the influence of the Brazilian left-wing parties because they have a close relationship with China. Jair Bolsonaro also wants to cut off ties with the Venezuelan government, which had a close working relationship with the ex-president Lula. Bolsonaro believes it is a socialist regime, and if Brazil wants to move forward, she should not have any place in her heart for a government that could influence the Brazilian people wrongly.

The influence of the leftwing deteriorated further as ex-president Lula was giving away Brazil's money to development projects in African nations and Cuba, while his own country was starving and did not have proper medical care and educational institutes. Bolsonaro, on the other hand, has given money to the less fortunate who have been impacted by the global COVID-19 crisis despite the Brazilian State Bank not having the capital to sustain their economy.

Now all of these policies of the right-wing are making the leftist parties, especially the Workers Party, very nervous because of their declining influence. But the Workers Party does not have the right leadership to gain momentum, and the recent policies of Jair Bolsonaro will make the right-wing parties of Brazil the right choice for the people.

As we come to an end, the Workers Party and its influence on Brazilian politics over the years is something for you to decide. Whether you think of it positively or negatively, it is a choice you make. But do understand that your undertaking of the policies will impact your future.

# Chapter 5: The Communist Parties

*"How do you tell a Communist? Well, it's someone who reads Marx and Lenin. And how do you tell an anti-Communist? It's someone who understands Marx and Lenin."* - **Ronald Reagan**

When he was in office, Ronald Regan was called the hawk by the last leader of the Soviet Union, Mikhail Gorbachev. He earned his name because of his views on communism. Regan was the one who asked Gorbachev to tear down the Berlin wall as the communist state was separating families who lived in the same cities.

Communism is a disease that can rot rice fields, cause a wildfire, and collapse entire civilizations. Brazil, having suffered for so long, chose socialism as they felt this was their only hope. But, if they had seen the condition of Cubans and friends in Venezuela, after choosing socialism, how there was no freedom of speech and no internet, they would have perhaps chosen something else. However, I don't blame them. I also voted for ex-president Lula, as I believed he was here to change Brazil for the better. I was wrong back then. Now, I hope Brazilians are not wrong in choosing a president who will be like Regan, for he is against the people who are determined to destroy Brazil. Keeping the intention of Brazil's betterment in mind, let's discuss how President Jair Bolsonaro is fighting socialism.

## Bolsonaro's claim to liberate Brazil from Socialism

In his inauguration speech, President Jair Bolsonaro claimed he had liberated Brazil from Socialism while the other parties spread their fake ideologies. The other parties were looting Brazilians off their wealth, which was their hard-earned money. He wants to end the crime wave that has been shaking Brazil.

Jair Bolsonaro is everything. The media portrays him negatively, though I firmly believe that President Jair Bolsonaro is a man of his word, and he would do as he said.

When he was elected, the whole of South America was chanting, 'change is coming.' When millions of people living in Brazil rejected Socialism, they were saying that enough is enough! President Jair Bolsonaro is here to liberate us! When it comes to socialism, South America is one of the worst continents in the world, as the people living here have always supported socialism. They do so as they are poor, uneducated, and don't know who to trust. This was the problem in Cuba as well. Many of the Cubans thought that since the United States was supporting Fulgencio Batista, he was not the ideal choice.

He was the person deemed responsible for inviting the Mafia to establish their illegal businesses in Havana and other cities around Cuba. For Cubans, Fidel Castro was the man who would have freed them from a leader selling them out. This was the problem in Brazil as well. Brazilians also thought that Lula was the best choice. It was only discovered after the elections that he was no different than Rousseff. However, when Brazil elected Bolsonaro, they showed their disapproval of corruption. Brazilians rejected the life of poverty and criminal activities. Brazilians want to improve the country's economy; they don't want to be another Venezuela that ranks last in America when it comes to the economy.

The Venezuelan currency no longer has the same value that it did a decade ago. Its government is hanging on to power, with protesters on the streets demanding change. These problems, however, can't be solved by an administration that is no longer respected by its citizens. Venezuela's collapse was witnessed by the world. The present happenings in Brazil are also being witnessed by every country in the world especially those in South America. When Brazilians elected a Far-Right leader, it was a message to Venezuela and Cuba that change was coming, and their time was up. Brazil realized the path towards socialism was leading them towards their destruction.

Look at Brazil; she chose a socialist leader, Lula. He made grand promises. He was helping the poor, but that was just a disguise to hide his true nature – the nature of a corrupt man. Lula's only intention was to spread his ideologies. Lula was not even spreading socialism or communism. Lula was creating his ideologies by the name of "Lulism," which at first seemed to work as it was helping the local businesses, communities, banks, and other industrial and social institutes around Brazil. But as the people of Brazil looked closer, Lula was not trying to save the country. He was selling it to communists like Cuba and China. So the speech that Bolsonaro had given was sending a strong message against socialism and corruption. Brazilians, being tired of the fake promises that were made about how they thought they could control everything, decided to put a stop to it all after hearing the speech. That is when things started to turn around.

President Jair Bolsonaro had policies that may seem similar to US President Donald Trump's policies. But Bolsonaro can turn Brazil into an economic powerhouse. Bolsonaro is trying to privatize all the companies that the state owns by removing people running these companies through their political connections. Like I mentioned in the previous chapter, when Lula and Rousseff were in power, relations with the United States deteriorated, but Bolsonaro has promised that he would strengthen the relations with the United States.

When President Trump came into power in 2016, many people in the US were tired of how the Democratic Party was leading the country. They wanted change, and when Donald Trump first announced that he would put America first, they elected him. I believe that is what happened in Brazil too.

All previous administrations in Brazil have failed. Some did try to change the system that created these problems, but when the system failed, it became impossible to change. Those who have created this system are corrupt and powerful. They are greedy. This was the system that Lula created, which led him to jail. Bolsonaro, on the other hand, is trying to clean the mess that Lula made.

Even Bolsonaro agreed that the only reason he got elected was that people were tired of the corruption done by the Socialist government. This is the reason why the young generation of Brazil is leaning towards the Far-Right Parties. They are supporting a guy who proudly supports anti-establishment. Still, his fight with the socialist party is not going to be an easy one. Ever since Bolsonaro came to power, the Workers Party have refused to acknowledge Bolsonaro's effort in improving the economy. Even the Left-Wing politicians sitting in the United States are falsely accusing him and claiming he is not the right leader for Brazil.

Even the ex-mayor of Sao Paulo, Fernando Haddad, mentioned that Bolsonaro is not a good leader for Brazil. Now, a man who has been accused of taking bribes from a construction company is accusing Bolsonaro of cleaning the system that he corrupted. Sounds ironic. Fernando Haddad is a member of the Workers Party that is one of the most corrupt political parties in Brazil and South America. They can't stand the thought of Bolsonaro accomplishing all that they wished to do in a short span of time.

The above is just one scenario that proves how socialism failed Brazil. Many Brazilians are adapting to these changes. With Bolsonaro in power, Brazil's economy is going to improve, which was growing until the Covid-19 pandemic struck the country. Although, it is believed that despite the pandemic, the economy, along with Brazil's relationships with many democratic governments, will improve. The crime rate throughout is estimated to drop, which was created by a government that did not care about its people.

Bolsonaro is trying to change the system, yet he has been compared to Donald Trump. This has made him a target of the lean-leaning media and the Workers Party. And not just the media but many politicians are comparing the two leaders, claiming they both will ruin their countries. But how can two people who put their countries first be bad for the residents living in their respective countries?

## How Bolsonaro is viewed as Brazil's Donald Trump

Both Donald Trump and Jair Bolsonaro came to power as the people were angry with the previous administrations. Bolsonaro and Trump are the same. They both are leaders who support Far-Right ideologies and are portrayed negatively in the media. Each uses Twitter to communicate with their followers and believes that people should be allowed to have guns to protect themselves. While this is insufficient to deem Bolsonaro to be the same as trump, since Bolsonaro was called the "Tropical Donald Trump," Trump started to admire him more. Donald Trump believed the relationship between the current administrations of Brazil would improve the bilateral relationship between the two countries.

However, my question here is that if both are the same, is it a good thing, as the trade between the United States and Brazil will improve? If this is the case, it means having the best economies in America, the United States and Brazil can move forward from any differences in their relationship. At the same time, Bolsonaro and Trump are worried about the crisis in Venezuela. This also shows that Donald Trump and Jair Bolsonaro's foreign policies are similar. They have the same view of the world.

When President Jair Bolsonaro visited the United States last year, he was warmly welcomed by President Donald Trump. During his visit, they both agreed that they would get along quite well. They both care about family values, faith in God and were attacked by "fake-news" media. Like Trump, Bolsonaro is not afraid of the media. He is an outspoken President who says what he likes. Trump and Bolsonaro equally hate the media for spreading rumors that can lead to the downfall of governments.

During the current Venezuelan crisis, both Trump and Bolsonaro support Juan Guaido. They think that Nicolas Maduro is a dictator who does not care about his people. Last year, during the height of the crisis, Brazil, with the assistant of the United States, tried to deliver aid to Venezuela. However, Venezuelan President, Nicolas Maduro, intervened. He thought it was a plan by the US to invade his country. Maduro has always denied his country facing a humanitarian crisis, but he did accept help from Russia when Russia promised to deliver the aid. Despite losing the support of the general population, Maduro has remained in power because he had the backing of the army. Donald Trump and Bolsonaro have faced opposition parties who demanded their impeachment. Many politicians from Democratic Party in the United States think that Trump was elected because he was backed by Russia. Similarly, many politicians in Brazil think that because Bolsonaro has neglected his duties during the current pandemic, he is not the suitable choice to run the country.

Much like Donald Trump made his children his advisers, like Ivanka Trump and her husband Jared, Bolsonaro has also made his children his closest advisers. Bolsonaro's son, Eduardo Bolsonaro, is a member of the Brazilian Congress. Eduardo sits in the foreign relations committee as the de facto foreign minister of Brazil as his father appointed him to be an Ambassador to the United States. Still, Eduardo's plans were rejected by the Brazilian Congress, for they thought he was too close to the Trump family.

Even after this year's election, Bolsonaro has refused to accept Donald Trump's defeat. Bolsonaro has even refused to congratulate Joe Biden, even after other nations, including Brazil's neighboring countries, having accepted Joe Biden as the next president of the United States. Bolsonaro even agreed with the claims Donald Trump made about election fraud. Bolsonaro mentioned the same, but without using the word fraud. He mentioned there were outside forces that tried to shift the election in favor of Joe Biden. Even when Brazilian Congress speaker, Rodrigo Maia, tried to congratulate Biden, Bolsonaro scolded him. He said, "The election is not over until all the votes are counted, and until the claims about election fraud is solved." Since Donald Trump has lost the elections, and Joe Biden is set to take office soon, it will make Bolsonaro very nervous. Trump was his biggest supporter, after all, and Bolsonaro made his policies that were similar to Trump.

Summing all of this up, you must have learned why people consider Bolsonaro to be the Brazilian Donald Trump. The problem, however, does not lie in Bolsonaro's comparison with Trump. It lies in why Brazil chose the Far-Right or why Brazil picked Lula as its president. The problem is why Brazil allowed communism to grow in the first place. Understanding how Brazil was tired of communism, they decided to give Bolsonaro a shot.

The next point that I will share with you will allow a better understanding of why the shift happened.

## How Brazil Shifted Back To Communism

After witnessing Brazil being ruined by the elite circles of societies, she decided to revert to communism. That is why when the Russian Revolution began in 1917, Brazilians quickly accepted the Russian Communist Party ideologies. They thought this was their only way to survive. Communism grew in Brazil as there was a growing concern among the workers. There was unrest brewing among them. So, the concept of the communism revolution grew in the mind of the workers, the poor, and those who could not defend themselves from the rich and the powerful.

Since the start, whenever the communist was living in Brazil, they tried to go against the regime. They were always brutalized, but the more they were brutalized, the more their support grew, and the more they grew in their ideologies. Every time they tried to resist the terrorizing of the Brazilian government, they would find a way to get back to power. During the Cold War, the Brazilian Communist Party rose to prominence after many Brazilian didn't understand the logic behind the Cold war. Because of this, the Brazilian Communist Party and its alliance started spreading their ideologies to the poorer residents of Brazil as they were the uneducated most.

Not just this, they also tried to improve the working conditions. The communists tried to give more power to the ordinary working-class citizens. This made the political elite and the religious leader nervous, who started to threaten the workers and farmers supporting communism. This made the communist ideology spread further as the poorer community found it interesting. It was also because the Communists promised to free the land from the political elites.

The Communist ideals were growing because of the political elites, but some of these ideologies were wrong. The Communists were demanding for the land to be distributed equally among the Brazilian people. At first, it sounded like a good thing, but when looked at closely, many of the people were going to get the land they did not deserve. Many of these Brazilians did not even work on the land. If they would have worked on the land and the elite class had wronged them, then it would have made sense. But because of these ideologies, communism grew in the mind of the farmers and the workers. A few centuries ago, from the Cold War, many workers were decedents of former slaves who were brought from Africa. So it was a good thing for them that change was coming. From these ideologies, the workers and farmers created one of the biggest farmer movements in South America.

During the time of the Populist Republic 1945 to 1964, Brazilian politics was so nervous with the growing influence of the Brazilian communist party that for them to get elected, they had to promise land reforms and workers' rights. But in the year 1964, when the Brazilian elites and the country military conspired that a military lead government should lead the government, it ended all the rights of the farmers and the workers. When the military came to power, they banned the Brazilian Communist Party. But when the Military led government was needed in the year 1985, and the New Republic was created, the Brazilian Communist again emerged. They started to influence the minds of Brazilians with their fake ideologies, but they never won enough votes in the general election.

Even though they never came to power, it helped the Brazilian Communist Party in creating the Labor unions, which developed into the largest movement the country had seen in 1990. This helped spread the communist ideologies. Even though the communist could not seize power in Brazil, their ideologies got spread when the Brazilian Workers Party was in power. Although they were not communists, the worker's party was a left-wing political party that was similar in nature to the Brazilian Communist Party.

Even today, the Brazilian Workers Party and the Brazilian Communist Party promised equal rights. They promise to end deficiency and make the general income the same for all Brazilians. That is why, even when Jair Bolsonaro is in power, the Left-Wing politician still has a lot of support from the Brazilian people.

As a result, this had made the job difficult for not just Bolsonaro but for many Brazilians. And when it seems that Brazilians are trying to forget about past corruption, the communist and the socialists emerged time and time again. Therefore, from this chapter, I hope you understand that our current President is the right choice for the country. He has the best interest of the nation in his heart, and the real enemy is one who prefer corruption or a life of crime.

# Chapter 6: Dictatorship vs. Democracy

*"The difference between a democracy and a dictatorship is that in a democracy, you vote first and take orders later; in a dictatorship, you don't have to waste your time voting."* - **Charles Bukowski**

For many people, a democratically elected leader is better than a dictator since they get to choose the person who will lead them forward. But if they take their time and look closer, they will realize that both of them are the same. Both are power-hungry human beings who will only think about themselves rather than their countries. Brazilians have experienced the pros and cons of both democracy and dictatorship. We are a nation that has suffered at the hands of people who will choose power and wealth above everything else. Brazilians have seen dictatorship and democracy failing.

In both scenarios, Brazilians were to be blamed as they allowed power-hungry people to dictate them, to choose their lives for them.

Although, how did both governments fail? Before we understand that, we need to understand how dictatorship and democracy differ. In this chapter, I will talk about democracy and dictatorship, what their advantages and disadvantages are, and how they can change your lives.

## Dictatorship vs. Democracy

As I mentioned before, Brazil is a country that has experienced both dictatorship and democracy, and both leaders failed in their jobs. For Brazil, she has seen her military taking over the government in 1964. The military took over the power from Joao Goulart, who was the democratically elected President of Brazil. The military government, led by a military junta that controlled everything in Brazil, took over the power as they were afraid that Goulart, who was a left-wing president, would turn Brazil into another Cuba. With the support of the United States and major business and political elites, the military overthrew the government. The military dictatorship lasted until 1984 when Brazil elected its first democratic leader.

So what was about democracy that allowed dictatorship to take over?

## What is Democracy?

In a democracy, the people have the right to elect their leader and its administration. Since the people get to elect whomever they think is best for their country, they will take an interest in the man or woman they have elected, for they want to see whether they made the right decision. When someone gets elected democratically, they cannot pass any legislation on their own. They have to go to the parliament, which is also chosen by the people, and submit their policy to them. The parliament then decides if the policy will benefit the country or not.

Sometimes when a democratically elected government wants to pass a resolution that can change the country's history, they will not just go to the parliament or the senate, but they will also consider a referendum. A referendum helps the government establish whether its people would benefit from the resolution/policy they want to introduce.

The United States and India are two of the biggest democracies in the world. Ever since they gained independence, they have been electing their leaders. India first elected Prime Minister Jawaharlal Nehru. On the other hand, the United States first elected President George Washington. This was just the start of their democracy, which has become the symbol of freedom and hope.

However, much like Latin America losing its democracy, many of its countries have witnessed their government being overthrown by their military. This was done with the support of western powers. One of its examples is Chile, which saw its President Salvador Allende being ousted by Augusto Pinochet, a general in the army. The irony is that Pinochet was appointed general by Salvador himself. Pinochet took power because Salvador was the first President in Latin America who was a Marxist. This frightened the United States. If Salvador was to continue to stay in power, his ideologies would spread throughout the entire continent. Hence, they supported Pinochet thinking he was the perfect choice in leading the country with the right mindset. So, when people choose democracy, they know the background of the politician. They know who they are choosing to lead their country. The people will know all about the appointed leader's flaws, their personal lives, and whether they have any criminal record. If the democratically elected leader fails, it is not just the politicians' fault; it is the fault of the entire nation for electing a leader who failed them.

Brazil is one of those countries that have chosen democratic elected leaders who failed them consistently. Still, Brazil continues to elect its leaders democratically as they are still searching for the right person who will lead them to a better future.

Now let's look at dictatorship.

# What is a Dictatorship?

In a dictatorship, the power of the entire constitution is handed over to one man or woman. There is no freedom of speech, and the country has no opposition. The total control over the country's activities means there will be no resistance to the tyrant who will ruin the country. But that is only the negative image of a dictator. There are many examples where a dictator has done good for the country.

For example, Mustafa Kemal Ataturk was the founder of modern-day Turkey. He was considered a dictator by the international community, but he is regarded as a hero by the Turkish population. Mustafa removed the influence of foreign powers from Turkish politics. He made a lot of changes to the Turkish constitution, which allowed women voting rights in elections. Furthermore, he improved the education system of the country. While it is considered that only a democratic leader takes total control over the country's operations, a democratic leader can do the same. Some democratic elected leaders are considered dictators when they choose to suppress the opposition and remove freedom of expression. Despite these leaders having good intentions for their country, they will want to stay in power for a long period. For example, Lee Kuan Yew is considered one of the best examples of a democratically elected leader in the world.

He made Singapore into an economic world power, whose influence has benefited many countries. But his time in office was also controversial since he suppressed freedom of speech. The people were not allowed to talk about the government or its policies, even when it was not for their benefit. The opposition also felt like it was not getting the freedom to run its camping smoothly because of the law. The law suppresses anyone criticizing the government, which assisted Lee Kuan Yew in staying in power for a long time.

Brazil has also witnessed a president who wanted to stay in power indefinitely. His name was Getúlio Vargas, who was the President for two terms. The first was in 1934-1945. Getúlio was initially elected as an intern President from 1934-37, but became a dictator and stayed in power until 1945. His second term, in which he stood for elections and won them, led him to be the president from 1951-54. He did try to transform Brazil from a plantation-based economy to an industrial economy, which would have benefited the country enormously. Thus, while not all dictators are bad, it does not mean that they seize power unlawfully. That is why President Bolsonaro is the right choice to be elected as the President of Brazil. He was chosen by the people who were tired of the elite political class. These politicians thought they are above the law.

One more example of a dictator that has been shaking the political landscape of not just that particular country but the entire world is Kim Jong-Un. The North Korean dictator, whose family has been ruling the country for decades, happens to be an authoritarian leader. Kim Jong-Un suppressed freedom of speech and have threatened any country that tries to interfere in its internal affairs. Now that's just one example of a bad dictator, but there could also be positive outcomes of such governments

Concluding all of this, I believe even if Bolsonaro supports military dictatorship, he is supporting it because it will help Brazil get out of its current situation. After all, sometimes, what a country needs is an authoritarian government that can help the citizens start respecting the government.

All leadership has its pros and cons, and each style of government can turn out for the betterment of the government. There are chances that dictatorship might turn out in favor of Brazil. Though, to understand this, we must first understand its pros and cons in depth.

## Pros and Cons of Dictatorship and Democracy

Democracy and dictatorship are not so different from one another. Both have advantages and disadvantages. Sometimes countries think just because a democratic leader is coming into power through elections, it will bring prosperity to the country. On the other hand, countries always consider a dictator as a person who will only ruin the country. Dictators are deemed to be selfish and self-centered. Well, it is not necessary that the elected politician will not be corrupt or power-hungry, much like it is not necessary that a leader will seize power and overthrow the elected government. It is not mandatory for a dictator to not care about its people.

Like every leadership, democracy and dictatorship have their advantages and disadvantages too. So let's begin with the pros before we dive into the cons of democracy.

## Pros of Democracy
### Low levels of inequality

A democratically elected leader will make sure that his or her cabinet has diverse members of all religious or racial groups. In the 2018 Spanish General Elections, Spanish Prime Minister Pedro Sanchez announced forming a gender-equal cabinet. He now has 11 men and 11 females in his cabinet. It is for the first time that a nation has witnessed this happening, and all of this is possible because of democracy.

### Assurance of human rights

When you select a democratically elected government, it will make sure that the rule of law is implemented and obeyed. They will make sure there is no human rights violation occurring in their countries. Netherland is one of the prime examples of countries that care about human rights. According to research that was done on some 73 countries, the Netherland ranks number 1 when it comes to human rights. That is because Netherland respects democracy, and not just in their country but globally.

**Religious freedom**

In most of the countries where there is a democratically elected leader, they will allow religious freedom, which many people might not see in a country ruled by a monarch or dictator. The United Kingdom is a diverse nation. It has many racial and religious groups, so the government there makes sure every race and religion is respected by their people. In return, they also ensure that those groups also respect their citizens.

**Educational rights and opportunities**

Usually, in a democratic country, its leader will make sure that the citizens have basic and affordable education. Singapore is one of those countries where the government has prioritized education and made it affordable. Sometimes when a student is not able to afford the fees, the government will cover all the costs.

**Democracy gives people a feeling of participation**

In a democracy, the people select the government based on its policies. When they do so, people will feel a sense of responsibility in helping the government succeed. In 2016, the government of the UK wanted to leave the European Union. They didn't just go to the Parliament, they opted for a referendum, in which 52% of the population wanted the UK to leave the European Union, and the British Government respected their decision.

These are just the advantages of having a democratically elected government, but there are many disadvantages as well. Brazil is one of those countries that has seen its advantages in the early days of Ex-President Lula. But then it started to go wrong for the government and the ordinary people.

Now let's look at the cons of democracy.

# Cons of Democracy
## Democracy may slow down important decisions

Sometimes it will take too long to implement policies for a democratically elected government. They have to get it to pass in a parliament, and it could take time. This is a problem in many countries. They might have good governments, but their parliament could be frustrating. They will debate over the policy for months or even years, and even if the policy has been passed, it has to be altered to satisfy all the political parties in the country. This will not benefit the progress of the country, as while the citizens were waiting for the policy to be passed, its economy would have suffered.

## Political inefficiencies can get expensive

As mentioned above, the parliament sometimes takes too long to pass the policy, which can cost the country a lot when it comes to its economy. While the government was busy discussing what needs to be changed in its policy, there was no one running the country properly. This could mean there would be fewer foreign investments; the unemployment rate will increase, which will make the basic necessities products expensive. This has been the case with Brazil; Over the years, Brazilian's have suffered because their politicians were too busy arguing among them. The politicians overlooked the situation.

## Minorities may be left behind

Although there might be more rights for minorities in democracy, they might still be left behind. Many politicians look to support the race or religion that is in the majority because that is the group whose vote they need to win the elections. In Brazil, sometimes the politicians forget about the indigenous population of Brazil, who were the natives as they are in the minority. These natives would not make a difference in the outcome of the elections; hence, the politicians appeal to the majority of the population.

## Economic vs. social interests due to lobbying

Some powerful businessmen or women might have connections with powerful people in the government, so they can influence the overall decisions of the government policies. Sometimes this decision will not benefit the country as the government's policies have to be on a social basis. But because big organizations see this as a threat to their growth, they will use their influence to change the government's decision regarding some of its policies. In Brazil, many businessmen have influenced the government's decisions in the past. These businessmen or women are so powerful and influential that many politicians feel under pressure to obey them.

**Politicians may act in an opportunistic manner**

During their terms, many politicians look to benefit themselves or their families by resorting to corruption. This does not benefit the country. Many times when they are about to get caught, these politicians will always choose to put the blame on someone else to get re-elected. Many third-world countries witness this. Every other leader that they choose turns out to be corrupt. This is due to their corrupt political system, which doesn't change. The corrupt system continues to benefit politicians.

Let's look at the pros and cons of dictatorship now to fully distinguish between the two styles of ruling.

# Pros of Dictatorship
## Government Corruption Can Be Removed Immediately

Dictatorship is a one-man show. All the corruption in the country could be removed in a matter of days. Any policy or rule that has to be implemented does not have to be passed by the parliament. In most cases of dictatorship, the parliament has been dissolved. They want to end the corruption as quickly as possible because they know they have come into power the wrong way, and they might not be popular among the citizens. Thus, by removing something that the general population hates, they might gain some favor.

## Dictators Improve International Diplomacy Using Their Personality

Many dictators are often very good diplomats as they are well mannered and they know how to handle tough situations. The reason behind this is that most dictators hail from the military. There are many examples of African dictators having good relations with western leaders. This was because many of these leaders knew they needed the west's support for them to stay in power; hence, the African dictators made their foreign policies based on this.

## Dictatorships Provide More Stability

In a democracy, the leader is only elected for a few years and cannot provide much stability. But in a dictatorship where the leader stays in power for a long time, there will be more stability that can be beneficial for the country. The citizens and leaders will know what the other wants or hopes to achieve through the policies, which will be in the interest of the country.

## Government Resources Can Be Released Immediately

In a democracy, the parliament has to approve the funding that might be required urgently by the general public. But in a dictatorship, in case of a national emergency, such as a natural disaster, or a pandemic, the government will be able to release the funds without approval from the parliament. When a country has a dictatorship and it is facing a national emergency like Covid-19, its leader could take out the funds from the state bank and come up with a plan in identifying the areas that need the funds most.

### Crime Levels Decrease

In a democracy, the government has to follow the rule of law in implementing any policy to tackle crime, which might seem too lenient. Sometimes these policies can take time to become law as different political parties will have a different opinions about the bill. In turn, all of the opinions arising will lead to a delay in the bill being passed, and hence increasing the crime rate in the country. But in a dictatorship, the punishment is more severe. Most dictators don't follow the rule of law and can implement new policies to tackle crime without the approval of the parliament. An example of this is when the Philippines witnessed dictatorship, the crime rate in the country drop by 50%.

Brazil also has witness military dictatorship, and it has seen its pros in how it tackles left-wing politicians. By doing this, the military dictatorship helps Brazil not becoming another Cuba. But there were also disadvantages of a dictatorship, which we will look at.

## Cons of Dictatorship
### Dictators Can Rewrite the Laws at Any Time

In a democratically elected government, the citizens of that country will see fewer laws being implemented because of the parliament. Alternatively, when a country is being ruled by a dictator, it will witness new laws being implemented swiftly as they don't need approval from the parliament. At times the law could only benefit the dictator or those he favors, which can cause harm to the country. Many Brazilians thought that the military government was making laws that were not benefiting the country.

## Opposition Is Not Allowed to Exist

In a democracy, when the government is making a mistake in running the country, or its policies are not for the benefit of the country, there is always the opposition to support the ordinary people. But in a dictatorship, the first thing the dictator does is remove the opposition, so there is no critical opinion of the policy the dictator makes. The dictator is also afraid that if he does not suppress the opposition, they will stand up against his rule and start a revolution that can overthrow his government. In Brazil, during the military rule, there was a mass protest against the dictatorship as people were demanding democracy.

## The Dictatorship Can Lose Control If the Leader Is Removed

If the leader of a dictatorship is overthrown or dies, and he does not have any children or siblings, the government will lose control of the country. If they lose control of the country, it will increase the crime rate and collapse the economy. While some dictators plot against their government from collapsing in their absence, it can lead to internal political tensions among family members. A similar situation happened in North Korea. Kim Jong-Un assassinated his half-brother so that he would not challenge him for power. But because this is a dictatorship, the leader was not held accountable for the murder and got away with it. But if this was democracy and the rule of law would have followed, the leader would have been held accountable and put on trial for the murder.

## A Dictator's First Priority Is Remaining in Power

In many countries, the dictatorship will not allow anyone to challenge its authority. The dictator will make sure they stay in power, no matter the cost. When the Brazilian people came to the streets demanding democracy, the Brazilian military government suppressed them in hopes of staying in power. The government knew once they would be removed from power, the left-wing parties will take over the country and spread their ideologies throughout.

## Freedom of Speech is Restricted

In a democracy, there is freedom of speech, and you can say whatever you want about the government. But in a dictatorship, there is a restriction on freedom of speech or a complete ban. The Cuban government controls state television and monitors what the citizens have to say about the government. If the citizens say anything that is critical about the government or its policies, they will arrest that person. In Brazil, the military dictatorship did try to control freedom of speech, but that was their way of suppressing the left-wing parties in gaining ground in the local political circles.

Like many countries, Brazil has seen its policy-making and breaking the country. Brazilians have elected leaders who have lied to the people, they have seen their elected government overthrown twice and taken over by a dictator, but that too turned out to be a failure. Sometimes, I wish Brazil can have a political future where the people select the right leader who will not lie to them. I hope that President Jair Bolsonaro is a leader who can make Brazil great again, just like he has promised.

I shall leave the pros and cons for you to evaluate. If you have read them, I believe you can sketch out which mode of government would be better for Brazil. I feel democracy would work in favour of Brazil.

**The need for Democracy and its Importance**

Democracy is a way of telling people that they are free. It promises security, stability, and a better future. Democracy is for the people to elect a leader they think is more suitable for leading them forward. It is for them to make sure the leader they elected will fulfill all its promises and will make sure to achieve its entire goal, which his or her government has set for its term. But sadly, this is not happening around the world. Many countries have seen their democratic system failing because of corrupt and power-hungry leaders.

Many countries in the world are facing conflict or have faced some sort of civil unrest in the past. So after the conflict is resolved, the local authorities should not call in general elections too early because the people, who will participate in the elections, will be the same people who were responsible for starting the conflict in the first place. Like after the Bosnia war, the local authorities there, called in elections way too early, so what happened was that the people that were responsible for the conflict in the first place, were the one who was participating. And when this is the scenario, the people of that country will have no choice but to elect a man or woman who might be good for their country.

Many countries' democratically elected leaders are influenced by foreign powers; now, for me, that's not democracy. Because in a democracy, the government should be chosen by the people of that particular country, and when they don't get that choice, the people will not be bound with their leader. The bond between the leader and its citizen is very important to bring stability to the country. When they choose a leader, they choose one who is just like them.

Like for example, London Mayor Sadiq Khan was elected in 2016 because he came from an ordinary background. His parents were migrants who came to the UK for a better future, he also works from a young age, and so when he was elected Mayor of London, he understands the problem that ordinary people face. So he has a strong bond with the people living in London. I wish that was true for Brazil because we too elected a leader, Lula, whom we thought was good for the country, but he turns out to be corrupt.

But it doesn't mean that if Brazil has one corrupt leader, it should define how Brazilians are as a nation. Brazil has moved on and selected democratically elected leaders in the pursuit of progressing the nation. When Brazil looks at a country that has a dictatorship and Monarch, Brazilians will realize how lucky they are.

When I talk about Brazilian selecting a leader that turned out corrupt, I was talking about Ex-President Lula. For me, Lula was a man who defines democracy. He was a man who wanted to change the nation for the better and wanted to lead them forward. But sometimes, not just Lula but many democratically elected leaders can lose their way as they are blinded by greed and corruption.

Democracy matters as it reflects an idea of quality, liberty, dignity, and having an equal vote say in electing their government. But if we want to make democracy vigorous again, every country has to do new projects between its citizens and politicians. Democracy is not simply a question of structure; it is a state of mind, it is an activity, and part of that activity is honesty. Many politicians are not honest. If they can't do something they promised, they have to be honest with their citizens instead of lying to them.

Nowadays, the citizens of all the countries in the world are educated, they are healthier, and are learning about all events happening within their country and globally. Many countries are opting for democracy, as politicians are moving towards their people. They want to follow in their people's footsteps; they want to lead their country in how their citizens want them to.

However, if the general public wants the politician, to be honest, they need to allow them to be honest. The public has to stop pressurizing the politician if they failed to fulfill a promise made during election campaigns. At times, the situation can be different from when the politician started their journey. If the public does not understand its leader, the politicians will resort to dishonesty and deception.

Many times honesty is what most politicians lack, and especially the politicians from Brazil. But it is also part of the fault of the Brazilians. They are too busy trusting every word that comes out of the mouth of a politician, forgetting the politician is human too. Hence, the democracy of Brazil comes under threat. Some people blame President Jair Bolsonaro for the problems that Brazil is facing, but if Brazilians are to looks at its history, they will witness a history of corrupt and power-hungry leaders.

Brazil has witnessed how even dictators deceived them. It shall not be wise to completely disregard democracy in Brazil in such a scenario.

**The ongoing fight for Brazil's democracy**

There are people in Brazil who believe that just because President Jair Bolsonaro is in favor of the military, he will put the entire democracy of Brazil under threat. But for me, the real problem is the leaders of the past, like Lula and Rousseff. These leaders committed corruption, lied to their people, and invaded the country with foreign products from China.

Bolsonaro is a leader who is trying to save Brazil's democracy. After Operation Car Wash, the economic crises, and now the pandemic Covid-19, not only is Brazil in a tight spot because of these but Bolsonaro too. Some experts believe Bolsonaro policies will bring Brazil back in time to the Portuguese colonization of Brazil. While that was a time of chaos, it was a time when there were no Socialist or Left-Wing Parties.

The journey for President Bolsonaro was made difficult from the start. He was betrayed by a person he trusted the most. The betrayal was not by corruption but greed. The person who betrayed Bolsonaro is Ex-Justice Minister Sergio Moro, who was made famous when leading the investigation in Operation Car Wash. Sergio arrested many political elites, including Ex-President Lula and Ex-President Rousseff. Bolsonaro made him his Justice Minister, and he was his right-hand man. But Sergio got greedy and had a disagreement with Bolsonaro, after which he submitted his resignation.

This situation has made the job for the current administration more difficult. To add fuel to the fire, pressure from the left-wing party, who are seeing the current situation as an advantage to gain ground in the political landscape, has increased. If the Left-Wing Parties do manage to come back into power, it will be a fight between the Right-Wing Parties and Left-Wing Parties. It will be a huge loss for Brazilian democracy. Brazil is considered one of the best democracies in South and Central America, and if Brazil is losing its democracy, it will cause a chain of events. Some of the events can include a collapse in many other democratically elected governments in the continent.

As you can see, Brazilian democracy is under threat. The current pandemic is not going to make the job easy for Bolsonaro. The Brazilian economy will also be a big problem, for if it collapses, the Brazilian government will also collapse. It was the economy that has caused the previous government to fail in their jobs more than their corruption.

To sum it all up, it is not always the mode of the ruling, but the leaders who fail to justify either mode of governing.

I hope you have learned that neither democracy nor dictatorship can be bad for a country. All of it is subjective. Sometimes democratically elected leaders can also become dictators when they refuse to give up their seats. This is happening presently in Venezuela. Nicolas Maduro is refusing to give up his power to Juan Guaidó. This is damaging their country. Their citizens are suffering, and more importantly, the future of their democracy is under threat as Nicolas Maduro is acting like a dictator.

This chapter will let you reflect on how you should choose your leader. It should allow you to know the cons and pros of both dictatorship and democracy, and it will allow you to know how lucky you are to be living in a democracy. You have the freedom of speech, you have an opposition that will always support you, and more importantly, you have the choice to elect the entire government.

# Chapter 7: The Problems Leftist Face

*"Now, what is the left's worldview in general? What is it? If you had to attach not a philosophy but an attitude to a leftist worldview, it's one of pessimism and darkness, sadness. They're never happy, are they? They're always angry about something. No matter what they get, they're always angry."* — **Rush Limbaugh**

Whether in Brazil, the United Kingdom, Australia, or anywhere else in the world, the left-wing parties are always at fault with the government. For decades, people have placed their trust in the left-wing parties. They have come out to their support and sacrificed their lives for them. But what did the people got in return? Years of corruption, fake ideologies, and empty promises of equal rights. All that the people have seen is inequality. They take away the land of the people and give it to those who don't deserve it.

In such a scenario, what Rush Limbaugh said is right. The left-wing parties are never happy. They always remain sad and angry, and I believe that has been their main problem.

However, there is a reason behind the resentment that lingers within the left-wing parties. Do you know what that reason or those reasons are? No? Well, let me tell you.

Problems the Current Left-Wing Parties Have Faced

The left-wing parties have faced many problems since the start of the military dictatorship. Many left-wing parties had to go underground because the military had banned all political movements in Brazil. The military government spread rumors that the left-wing parties want to start a revolution. The reason was that during the Vargas administration, the left-wing parties used guerrilla tactics against the government. Because of these rumors, many people believed the government and the left parties lost their support.

During the military government, the left-wing party lacked the support of the business elites. The government thought if they were to support the left-wing party and brought them into power, the left-wing party will turn against them and take over their lands. The military ended up repressing the left-wing parties so they could not gain the support of the Brazilian people. As a result, the left-wing party suffered a major setback in 1969. This led to another catastrophic event. A communist group started a revolutionary movement on the 8th of October by kidnapping the United States ambassador, Charles Burke Elbrick. They kidnapped him as the U.S. was supporting the military government of Brazil.

All of this was just the start of their problems when the Workers' Party of Brazil was created; they started facing problems not only with the military administration but with other left-wing parties too. The Brazilian communist party wanted to follow the traditional ways of communism, and the Workers' Party wanted to revert from the old ways. This led to a tremendous amount of tension between the two parties.

Moving along as the left-wing party continued to face problems, ex-president Lula came into power in 2002. Many business elites assumed he would make the country a communist state, as Lula had told his supporters he wanted equality in Brazil. And even though Lula promised the left-wing party he was not against them, they did not trust him. As time went by, things deteriorated for Brazil. What Lula did in his presidency is known to the world. In 2008, an economic crisis took place where Lula told the Brazilian people not to be afraid. Lula consoled people that nothing will happen to the Brazilian economy. And it was the truth at that time. However, during the term of his protégée Rousseff, the Brazilian economy collapsed. The collapse was Lula's fault, as it was his ignorance that caused the crisis.

The problem started again during the Rousseff administration when she removed her chief of staff, Antonio Palocci. Antonio was removed over a corruption scandal by the name of the Mensalao scandal, though Rousseff remained popular during her first term. Nevertheless, during her second term in 2015, all of this changed. Due to the numerous scandals, her party was facing, like the Petrobras scandal, the main reason that contributed to her downfall was Jonathan David Taylor. Jonathan was a whistle-blower. He exposed how a Dutch company was responsible for giving hundreds of millions of dollars in bribes to top executives in Petrobras so they could have offshore oil reserve contracts. From there onwards, in 2016, Rousseff was impeached due to the corruption scandal and is currently serving a jail term.

Even after being convicted, Lula's supporters still believe their leader is innocent. What I have written above is a concise summary of all that happened in Lula's term. Despite all of that happened, people continue to support Lula. They believe all the corruption is just wild accusations hurled at Lula. Though, pause and ask, why was Lula given properties as gifts by senior executives from major companies?

A person, who people thought was a saint, turned out to be a devil who wanted to ruin the country. In 2017, a year before the 2018 general election, Lula was sentenced to 10 years in prison. However, when the authorities went to arrest him, they were met by strong resistance from the left-wing party politician. Because of this, Lula's sentence was increased to 12 years. In 2018, just months before the general elections, Lula surrendered.

Had it not been resistance from the left-wing parties, I believe Lula would not have been sentenced. Still, the left-wing parties are losing ground because of their ideologies of the past. They may have found success in the past, but as time is changing, many people now see them as a threat to democracy. In 2017, the Czech Republic, Italy, Austria, and France saw their left-wing parties losing ground to Far-Right parties. But one look at the left-wing parties' issues, the parties will be able to go back to the early stages of their formation. It is the early formation that was ruined by some corrupt leaders of the left-wing parties. And if a person, who may not be corrupt, follows the ideology of someone who was, he will give off the image of being corrupt too. This has to be changed so left-wing parties can gain the favor of the people again.

In 2020, many people were viewing the left-wing parties as too weak to handle. This is a problem that may require a swift and firm response.

## The Various Problems the Brazilian Left-Wing is Facing

The Brazilian Workers' Party is facing a lot of problems presently. When Lula was released from prison in 2019, he told his supporters the Workers' Party would defeat President Jair Bolsonaro in the 2022 general election. Lula was met with a skeptical response, even from his party. If he had said the same thing back in the 1990s or 2000s, his remark would have been met by a more positive attitude. The truth, however, has been laid in front of the people. The Workers' Party has been riddled with corruption scandals, more famously in the long-running investigation of the operation 'Car Wash,' which has witnessed some of the most powerful people in Brazil going to Jail.

The corruption scandal was not the only thing that has ruined the Workers' Party's reputation. During the presidential term of Lula protégée, Rousseff, Brazil faced a serious economic crisis, in which many people lost their jobs. This was the reason why Rousseff was impeached and was investigated for corruption, in which she was found guilty and sentenced to prison.

Since the 2018 general elections, the Brazilian Workers' Party has been in opposition. They performed poorly as they were facing the wrath of the people because of their own wrongdoing. Lula realized the Workers' Party was doing everything to regain the support Lula had from Brazilians. It still was not working for them.

Lula became an illness for Brazilian's. One they could not remove yet need at the same time. The Workers' Party was supposed to be the people's political party. Their ideology was supposed to help Brazilians from all corners of life, but it ended up becoming Lula Workers' Party. He transformed them into something entirely different from their origins.

As Lula heavily influenced the Workers' Party, the main problem is that the Workers' Party is more radical than it has ever been. Even their supporters are worried as they changed drastically. Their visions and goals seemed to have changed. This year, Brazil's Workers' Party hosted a convention that invited leaders from three socialist and communist states: Cuba, Venezuela, and Nicaragua. During the convention, when Lula was blamed for the corruption he did, Lula blamed the United States for the corruption allegation against him. Despite Lula being convicted and sentenced to 12 years in prison and his release next year, he blamed another country for his misconduct.

Presently, Brazil has no sound political party. Even when the Workers' Party is the only influential Left-Wing Party in Brazil, it lacks the leadership needed to defeat the Right-Wing president, Bolsonaro. The main problem being faced by the Workers' Party is that there are a lot of anti-sentiments against them. People no longer trust their leaders, and any leader from the Workers' Party standing for elections in 2022 will lose if they don't change their ideologies.

To add to the problems of the left-wing parties, Lula is making his comeback for the 2022 general elections. The senior members of the Workers' Party are reluctant to see Lula leading them again, but they don't seem to have a choice.

The problem with the Left-Wing Parties is that whenever they are in power, they don't want to focus on running the country smoothly. All they want to do is spread fake ideologies. Alternatively, all the other political parties, be it the Central-left, Central-Right, Central, and the Right-Wing Parties, don't try to spread their ideologies. These parties just focus on doing their jobs to get reelected in the next elections.

When Lula was in prison, Lula shifted their allegiance to the radical left to gain the support of the extremist left-wing supporters. Miraculously, it worked. But to achieve that, they lost a lot of support, especially from the business elites and other political elites. This was because of Jair Bolsonaro's cash handout program, which hammered the support of the poorer communities of Brazil for the Workers' Party.

It suffices to say that due to the Workers' Party's recent incompetency and lack of leadership, they have lost the support of Brazilian's. Nevertheless, the current Brazilian economic crisis due to the Covid-19 has handed a golden chance to the Workers' Party. The only problem is they lack the leadership to give them that chance.

Granted that a lack of leadership is leading to the defeat of the Left-Wing parties, this gives a chance to the far-right to win the next elections.

# Overthrowing Opposition to Stand a Chance

The Brazilian Far-Right is not going down without a fight. For them to win the general elections, Bolsonaro has to adopt the same approach that he used to win the 2018 general elections. Nationalism was the only thing that got Bolsonaro in power. People needed someone who could change the country by introducing new policies because they were tired of the Workers' Party and their policies. Not only this but also the support Bolsonaro received from the business elites, he will need it again to win. If Bolsonaro is elected, he has to bring in new policies. He has to change the system that was altered by the Left-Wing Party.

Bolsonaro did introduce industrialization. He tried to create jobs that can give the Brazilian economy boost, which will lower the crime rate. Similarly, Bolsonaro can try to gain support from the areas that were the stronghold of the Workers' Party. Because of the 2020 U.S. general elections, where Bolsonaro's biggest supporter was Donald Trump, he will now have to change his policies. Bolsonaro could no longer get the support of the U.S. president.

Bolsonaro has to unite the people of Brazil from all corners of life. He has to appeal to people that he is the right choice for them. He even has to go to the Left-Wing voters and ask them to change their allegiances. He has to change his ideologies a bit for them so they can see that he is the man for the people.

If Bolsonaro is defeated in the 2022 elections, it will be a major blow to all the nationalistic governments in the world.

Bolsonaro has to go back to his original roots, which was the support of the business elites, the Catholic Church, and the support of ultra-Far-Right Supporters. Since March of this year, his rating is going up after Bolsonaro introduced a financial aid package. The financial aid package helped all those families who lost their businesses or jobs. He will need to continue on this path if he hopes to defeat the opposition, which will be led by the Workers' Party. While the Workers' Party is facing setbacks due to their ideologies, the only thing in their favor is the opposition rising against Bolsonaro globally. If Bolsonaro can tackle the opposition against him coming from international media, the Workers' Party will continue to be at a disadvantage.

The following problems Brazil has faced recently do play a factor as well in overthrowing the opposition. Let's have a look at them:

## Economic Crisis

Brazil's Economic crisis was already happening before Bolsonaro came to power. The root cause for all of this is the administration of ex-president Rousseff. She mishandled the economic situation Brazil was facing. In 2015 and 2016, the Brazilian economy was already shrinking, and it was getting worse. When Bolsonaro came into power, the opposition placed the entire blame on Bolsonaro and his administration. Presently, Bolsonaro is trying to create jobs by introducing industrialization and agricultural industries in Brazil, which is looking good, because as November was a record on employment wich more than 400.000 new people get their official jobs, "carteira de trabalho," not just "bicos" (handy man).

## Amazon Rain Forest Fire

When the Amazon fires started last year, the world blamed Bolsonaro. The environmental NGOs blamed him for burning the forest, claiming he wanted to use the land for industrialization. Through all of this, only the French President, Emmanuel Macrons, commented on the Amazon fire, as Brazil is their colony. Where the whole world was blaming Bolsonaro, he was busy sending the military to fight the fire while facing the backlash of the international community. This is seen as an opportunity by the left-wing parties to further destabilize their place in the next presidential elections. But Bolsonaro reacts firmly, saying that Amazonas is our business. Have you taken care of your forest before? Then shoot up!

## COVID-19

While the entire world was imposing lockdowns, Bolsonaro didn't want to harm Brazil's already fragile economy. The economy was fragile because of the corruption done by the previous administration and the Amazon Rain forest fire, which was making foreign business investors nervous. What added fuel to the fire was that the current pandemic was affecting the export of Brazil. The scarcity of resources and instability of the market was a constant threat to Brazil's sovereignty. Hence, Bolsonaro didn't agree to impose lockdown, which was seen as an opportunity by the opposition to move to the impeachment plans against Bolsonaro.

**Media**

Bolsonaro has been strong and vocal about the media's role in creating an unstable condition of the economy, the Amazon Fire, and the COVID-19 pandemic. He states the media is creating a negative image of him for the world to see. This is to the extent where the European Union summoned the G7 summit to discuss the Amazon Fire. It was because the media was blaming Bolsonaro for the fires and portraying him as the oppressor of the indigenous people of Brazil. However, Bolsonaro stood fast and showed the world and his media that he couldn't be bullied and intimidated by them. However, all of this only worked against him. The opposition had used this to gain supporters. The opposition has been spreading propaganda against Bolsonaro with the help of the media, which creates uncertainty for Bolsonaro when it comes to elections.

As we come to the end of this chapter, the left-wing might be facing problems; yet, they are using their incompetency against Bolsonaro. Their previous flaws are being put on Bolsonaro via fake news. From the Amazon Rain forest fires to the Covid-19 pandemic and even the problems they created, such as the 2014 economic crisis, everything seems to be twisted, so it is perceived as Bolsonaro's fault.

Nevertheless, Bolsonaro has been fighting on all fronts and still managing to push Brazil forward, especially in sectors like agriculture and industrialization. The world must realize and see that the real problem is not Bolsonaro but the left-wing parties. If only the left-wing parties would stop spreading fake ideologies and propaganda, they can lead to the success of not just Brazil but the whole of South America. Still, the only person who seems to be doing that is their opposition, Jair Messas Bolsonaro.

# Chapter 8: Bilateralism

*"Foe means enemy. Now, will we have differences of opinion with the Russians? Yes. Will they get mad at us from time to time, and we get mad at them? That's part of the normal diplomatic relations."* -*Colin Powell*

A bilateral relationship is one of the most fundamental responsibilities for Brazil or any other country in the world. Countries must maintain a healthy relationship with their neighbors as countries share common economic and cultural goals, leading to a stable region.

From time to time, countries might have had a shaky relationship that led to a fragile relationship with other countries. As Colin Powel said, countries might have their differences when it comes to their opinion, ideologies, and methods in which they want to deal with a certain problem. However, it is normal when it comes to diplomatic relations.

Likewise, as Brazil is considered a regional power, they have to ensure a good and healthy relationship with the numerous regional powers in the world. For example, in Asia, Brazil should focus on having a good bilateral relationship with India, South Korea, Japan, and Taiwan. In the Middle East, Brazil should focus on building a good relationship with Israel, Saudi Arabia, and the UAE.

The current Brazilian administration of President Jair Bolsonaro's foreign policies, including having a good and healthy relationship with the United States, became fragile during Ex-President Lula and Ex-President Rousseff's time. As mentioned before, Brazil is considered a regional power; thus, Brazil has to send a message not just to the United States but to other countries as well. That message will portray that Brazil will have a good and healthy relationship with other countries, as long as they respect Brazil's culture, ideologies and won't interfere in Brazil's internal matters.

In the past, there was a scenario where the previous Brazilian administrations did contribute to turning Brazil into a regional power. Still, they didn't stop other countries from interfering in Brazil's internal matters. The previous Brazilian administration didn't stop Cuba from spreading its fake ideologies. The previous Brazilian administrations didn't stop China from taking over the Brazilian market. Unlike the previous administrations, however, Brazil comes first for Jair Bolsonaro. He has a diplomatic relationship with those countries that respect Brazil.

Keeping Brazil's relationship with global countries in mind, let's discuss why a bilateral relation is essential for Brazil.

## Brazil as a Regional Power

Brazil is considered a regional power by the international community at the start of the 21st century, or for some countries, an emerging regional power that has the ambition to grow their influence beyond the USA. But the problem is, in which region can Brazil increase its power? After all, in Latin America, Mexico is already considered an emerging regional power. In the Caribbean and Central America, the United States has a strong influence. That leaves Brazil and South America, though, throughout its history, Brazil has always had a hard time maintaining a good relationship with the United States. That makes it hard for Brazil to have a good relation with South American countries as South America is influenced by the USA in recent years.

During Brazil's Independence declaration in the year 1870, famous Brazilian words were, "We are of America, and we wish to be Americas." Nevertheless, as years passed and Brazil became a Republic in 1889, they established a stronger relationship with their South American neighbors by fixing the numerous problems Brazil was facing. Brazil's primary focus was having a good relationship with Argentine and Chile because of their shared cultural values.

During the same period, they tried to have a closer relationship with the United States. During that time, the USA and Brazil were considered two of the emerging regional powers. One other reason that the two countries were pushing towards a diplomatic relationship was the Spanish Empire. The Spanish American government was tired of the United States continuously interfering within the Spanish colonies of Mexico, Central America, and the Caribbean, which started towards the end of the 19th century and the 20th century.

The Spanish government even started to suspect the USA when they started to invest in its colonies and started to influence some of the political leaders through Pan-Americanism. On the contrary, it was not the case with Brazil. The Brazilian government did share the same values as the

Spanish government, whereas the Spanish government did not have similar ideologies and goals as the US government.

During the eight meetings from the year 1889 to 1938, the Brazilian government fully supported the US. Even when the US declared war against Germany during World War One, Brazil was the only country that supported them. And despite not having an active part during World War Two, Brazil again gave its full support to the US government and was one of the most important allies of the US among its neighboring countries.

The US first came to recognize Brazil as an essential part of the American continent. And this view was solidified during the US's ex-president Roosevelt's time both during World War Two and the Cold War. The reason behind this was that the US's economy was under threat with the growing influence of Fascist regimes in Europe during World War Two and then during the Cold War. The growing influence of the Soviet Union started to interfere with the US economy and its political plans for the region.

Brazil had always supported the US during the Pan-American meetings, World War Two, and the Cold War. Regardless, it was bitterly disappointing that the US government didn't consider Brazil a special friend since they didn't treat Brazil fairly. Even though Brazil remained a good ally of the US and the west during the Cold War, from the year 1961 to 1964, Brazil started to amend its foreign policy, whose main focus was to have a good relationship with Cuba. At that time, Cuba was going through a revolution led by Fidel Castro, China, and other underdeveloped nations, with countries from Africa and Asia.

The Brazilian government at that time started to support many countries that were getting tired of colonial powers.

The Coup of 1964 was backed by the US, which saw the Brazilian military taking over power lasting for 21 years. Even then, there was tension and disagreement between the two nations. Brazil's foreign policies often supported third-world countries, which fueled up the tension with the US even more. It was due to the US's interests in some of those countries, like the Middle East and Africa.

In the Americas, it was becoming clear that Brazil, whose population was 35 million in the 1930s, grew to 170 million by 1980. With that, the Brazilian economy also grew. Still, Brazil had no intention of becoming a world power. It definitely didn't want to become a peacemaker in the region for the US, crashing the hopes of the US State Department, which was planning to ask Brazil to do exactly that.

In the year 1980, Brazil's relationship with its historical arch-rival and neighbor, Argentine, dramatically improved after it decided to join the Association for Latin American Integration, also known as ALADI. One of the main reasons was that both Argentine and Brazil elected democratically elected leaders in the mid-80s, which led to the Treaty of Asuncion of the year 1991. That treaty created the Mercosur trade bloc, which was made up of Brazil, Argentine, Uruguay, and Paraguay. In the later years, more countries joined the organization, including Chile and Bolivia.

After nearly 40 years from the end of World War Two, Brazil didn't have a really good relationship with its neighbors despite Brazilian poets, celebrates, writers, and activists starting to identify themselves as Latin American, especially those who were following left-wing ideologies. Truth be told, many people, even among the Brazilian population, didn't consider Brazil a part of the Latin American community as Brazil's official language is Portuguese; many of the nations in Latin America speak Spanish.

After the end of the Cold War, Brazil saw its economy increasing. That bought in a shift in the political structure of Brazilian politics as Brazil first stabilized its democracy, then improved its economy. Because of this, Brazil had a huge influence on the world. It started to grow under the ex-president Fernando Henrique's rule, who was Brazil's President from the year 1995 to 2002.

Brazil continued to grow under ex-president Lula's term, where Brazil saw a very close relationship with Cuba, Venezuela, China, and other third-world countries. Alternatively, under the current President, Jair Bolsonaro's term, Brazil had grown closer to the United States regardless of their past rocky relationship as both wanted to consolidate their influence in the region and become the only regional power.

All of this is sure to set multiple perceptions about Brazil and the kind of relationship it establishes with the world. Now there are a lot of countries that view Brazil differently. For the US, Brazil was viewed as an economic and political partner that has similar goals. At the same time, China is one of those countries that have a huge influence on the Brazilian economy. Then there are Brazilian neighbors who have their own opinion about Brazil. In my next point, I will be discussing how other countries view Brazil and how that has influenced Brazilian foreign policy.

## Brazil's View on the International Stage

When Lula was in power, 24% of Brazilian thought that Brazil was a world power, and 53% thought that it would become a world power. But there was a small portion of Brazilians who thought that Brazil could never become a world power under ex-president Lula's administration. While many people thought that Lula was having a positive impact on the country, some thought Lula was harming the nation.

Many Brazilian wanted their country to have a positive impact on the global stage. Although Brazilians also knew for a fact that Brazil still had a long way to go before it became a global power. Brazil has been considered the leader among its neighbors because of its military, economic strength, and foreign policies. Brazil also has a long history of making its economy part of its foreign policy, which has benefited its neighboring countries while strengthening their relationship with Brazil.

Brazil is the founding member of the Organization of American States, also known as OAS, and the Inter-American Treaty of Reciprocal Assistance, which is also known as the Rio Treaty. Thus, Brazil always considered its neighbor an essential part of Brazilian foreign policies. One of the prime examples of this is that Brazil supports different organizations in South America like the Latin America Integration Association (ALADI), The Union of South American Nations (UNASUR), and Mercosur, which is the common trade market in South America. Even though Brazil wants to help these organizations, Brazil also has a hidden agenda. Through this organization, Brazil wants to have a global impact on its neighbors, from whom they can make policies that can influence the entire region. Thus, it will assist Brazil in cementing its role as a regional power.

Brazil wishes to influence South American countries; they want to spread their influence to the wider world, which includes Central America and the Caribbean. But the problem is Brazil always had a fragile relationship with this part of the region, and many experts believe that Brazil's attempt in influencing this region will be futile if another regional power emerges. Brazil made headlines a few years ago after it successfully hosted the 2014 Football World Cup and the 2016 Summer Olympics. Although, after those events, Brazil's reputation was tarnished in the global arena.

First was the collapse of the Brazilian economy, until that point was considered one of the best in the world. Then it was the corruption scandal known as operation-car wash, which further sent a negative image of the country. The damage Brazil incurred at the expanse of defamation is something Jair Bolsonaro wants to eradicate. The administration of Jair Bolsonaro is trying to clean up the mess the previous administrations made. He wishes to send a message to its neighbors and the wider world that Brazil is still a regional power. However, Jair Bolsonaro's attempt to undo the doings of the previous presidents will require time and effort, and importantly the support of Brazilian's.

Ex-president Lula was in power from 2002 to 2010, during which the Brazilian foreign policies went through considerable changes. Brazil, whose relationship with the US was good during the military administration era, worsened.

What led to that? Well, Brazil had a very good relationship with some of the left-leaning countries like Cuba, Venezuela, and China. So let's discuss a bit about the foreign policies Lula made.

## Foreign Policies of Lula

As mentioned before, since 1985, Brazil's foreign policies went through massive changes, for Brazil realized it had a golden opportunity of becoming a regional power. This became possible during the term of ex-president Fernando, who was Brazil's president from 1995 to 2002. His administration first thought that Brazil should influence the global stage, which later turned out to be for Brazil's benefit.

As time progressed and ex-president Lula adapted that policy, changes started to emerge for the worse. During the term of Lula, Brazil's diplomatic relationship improved with African countries. During his two years, these included trade-deal being signed with some of the regional powers in Africa. The investments were carried out by the Brazilian business community among the third-world countries in Africa.

Consequently, Brazil is now carrying out political dialogue to help strengthen Brazil's relationship with these countries. Many new embassies were opened during the Lula presidency, making Brazil the fifth country with the most diplomatic mission in the entire African continent. Lula also visited 23 countries during his two terms. Brazil opened an office for the Brazilian enterprise to help with agriculture reforms named EMBRAPA in Ghana. There were many other Brazilian corporations opening in numerous African nations, like a pharmaceutical company in Mozambique. Lula's administration sent people to the African countries to train Brazilian farmers in the agriculture industry, like the cotton and rice industries.

There were many downsides to Lula's foreign policies. For example, when he refused to provide farm subsidies and refused to sign an agreement of a Free Trade Agreement of Americas, also known as FTAA, it led to the failure Cancun World Trade conference in 2003 called by the G8 nations. On one hand, the conference did not result well. On the other, Lula had a good relationship with Venezuela and Colombia, helping both countries solve their internal matters. Lula also tried to maintain a relationship with the US's ex-president George Washington Bush. Through this, Lula tried to tell the world that he is not trying to spread his ideologies and that he was just doing these to improve the Brazilian diplomatic relationship. However, even though he was improving Brazil's diplomatic relations with other countries, he was also stealing billions of dollars from the Brazilian people, which he used to develop other countries. Lula used that money in helping Cuba to build a port when millions of Brazilians didn't have the basic medication, education, and even food.

When ex-president Rousseff came into power, the relationship with the United States was almost ruined. This was followed by the next administration of ex-president Michel Temer. The corruption scandal made Jair Bolsonaro's job even more difficult because he had to re-establish Brazil's reputation in the international circle.

With all the excess baggage worth of damage left behind by previous presidents, Jair Bolsonaro is now trying to fix Brazil's foreign policies, which would benefit Brazilian's.

## How Jair Bolsonaro is trying to improve Brazil Bilateral Relationship

When he was campaigning in 2018, Jair Bolsonaro told the media that he would change the Brazilian foreign policies in favor of Brazil. He also said that Brazil should stop idolizing countries with dictators, and they should admire countries like the US, Italy, and Israel. Jair Bolsonaro also views the US, Israel, Japan, South Korea, and Taiwan as positively influencing Brazil. Bolsonaro also wants to distance himself from China, which he blames for taking over Brazilian markets. When he became President, he told the Brazilian people that he did want to continue doing business with China, but with a better trade agreement that would benefit both countries. Bolsonaro also admired President Donald Trump's foreign policies and has made similar foreign policies, especially in Iran and Venezuela. He is also considering moving the Brazilian embassy from Tel

Aviv, a move that has to strengthen the relationship between two of the region's greatest power. Even the former Security Adviser of the US admired President Jair Bolsonaro because of the similarities in the two administrations' policies.

When it comes to having a closer tie with a regional leader, Jair Bolsonaro said that he admired Argentine's President Mauricio Macri, who ended the 12 years term of Nestor and Cristina. Bolsonaro considers these two similar to Rousseff and Lula. Bolsonaro even has mixed views about Mercosur. On one side, he doesn't want to leave the organization. On the other, he thinks that the organization helps the leaders spread their fake ideologies that can harm various countries' local economies, especially Brazil.

In 2020, Jair Bolsonaro visited India during their Republic Day Celebration in Delhi, where he was the Guest of Honor. He also promised his counterpart, Narendra Modi, the prime minister of India, to support India for the permanent seat in the United Nations Security Council. Both of their countries are one of the biggest economies and democracies in the world. And in the same year, he also visited the US, where he was welcomed by President Donald Trump. Both presidents discussed the current situations in the Middle East and the Americas.

Bolsonaro further backed the US's effort to remove the current President of Venezuela, Nicolas Maduro. He also wanted to have a closer military corporation with the US. Bolsonaro also requested the US government to support Brazil's bid to become a permanent NATO member.

Bolsonaro had a closer tie to the Trump administration. Therefore, he was comfortable dealing with the US. However, it is going to change since Donald Trump lost the 2020 election in November. Bolsonaro had a shaky relationship with the incoming US President, Joe Biden.

Times change, and so do policies. Where previous leaders were inept in adapting to changing political situations, Bolsonaro is striving to do the opposite. President Jair Bolsonaro had to make changes in his foreign policies when it came to dealing with the United States. He will have to do the same since he will now be dealing with a different administration whose ideology is different from Jair Bolsonaro. Let's look at how Joe Biden's policies can influence Brazil.

## How Joe Biden Victory can change Brazil Foreign Policy

Usually, the US election doesn't attract much attention in Brazil. Still, the 2020 United States election did make it into every newspaper in the country. That was because of President Jair Bolsonaro, an ally of US President Donald Trump, who prompted Bolsonaro to change his foreign policy to align with his. When Bolsonaro visited the White House in 2020, he told the US media that he believes Donald Trump will be re-elected for four more years. Things, however, turned out differently.

Now that Joe Biden has been elected as the next president of the United States, Bolsonaro has to change his foreign policies. That can be a huge problem for him since Bolsonaro had a shaky relationship with Joe Biden.

When Joe Biden was campaigning for the elections, he had told the media when he would take over the White House, he would give $20 billion to end the Amazon rainforest fire. Joe Biden also added that Brazil did not do anything to fight the fire; hence, he would impose sanctions on Brazil. In response, President Jair Bolsonaro tweeted that Amazon is part of Brazil's Sovereignty and that Joe Biden can't threaten him or the Brazilian people. That is the reason why Bolsonaro didn't acknowledge Joe Biden's victory in November's election and told the media that he would wait until the official result is announced.

One month after Joe Biden's victory, Bolsonaro did accept Joe Biden, and he told him he was ready to work with the current US administration. Ernesto Araujo, the current Brazilian foreign minister, even started to make changes to Brazil's foreign policies. He is ready to work with the in-coming United States Secretary of State Antony Blinken, replacing the out-going Mike Pompeo, who had a closer relationship with the Brazilian foreign minister. However, some people believe since Joe Biden and Bolsonaro had a shaky history, this will prompt the Brazilian president to have a good relationship with China - Brazil's largest trading partner.

With a new administration in the White House, Bolsonaro's work has been cut out for him. He will still try to maintain a good diplomatic relationship with the incoming US administration. Still, for this, sacrifices have to be made on both sides.

As we come to the end of this chapter, I hope you realize now that a bilateral relationship is essential for any government. If we don't have a good relationship with other countries, there will be a lack of trust in the administration from the global community. For example, North Korea is one of the most isolated countries in the world, with having a good relationship with only Russia and China. On the other hand, Singapore has a diplomatic relationship with almost every country in the world.

What is the difference? North Korea has suffered from international sanctions as the global community doesn't trust them. They also do not receive any assistant from any other country. One of the reasons for this is that the North Korean government prefers to isolate its own country. On the other hand, Singapore has a good relationship with other countries. They have a good relationship with almost every country in the world, and that is why their citizens are welcomed in almost 190 countries without a visa. That makes the Singaporean passport one of the strongest in the world. Singapore also had one of the busiest ports in the world. This is because the Singapore government wants to have a good bilateral relationship with other nations, which will boost its economy.

Similarly, if Brazil wishes to have good ties with the world, it will have to work towards harboring such a relationship first.

# Chapter 9: Nationalist Movement

*"Nationalism cannot flower if it does not grow in the garden of internationalism."* -**Sukarno**

Nationalism is an ideology that defines the love a leader has for his country, a country where he was born, a country whose culture and people are in his roots; Nationalism is something that very few leaders have. Like Indonesia's first President, Sukarno said, Nationalism cannot blossom if it does not grow in the garden of internationalism. Similarly, for Nationalism to blossom, any country has to have a good relationship with its neighbor. It is essential. It is the fundamental duty of a leader to have good relationships with every country in the world. Still, it is also the fundamental duty of a leader to put his country first. For me, this is the true meaning of being a nationalist.

Brazil has seen leaders who differ in ideologies; their ideologies differ because they come from different backgrounds. At first, some of these leaders might have the right ideas. They might also seem like the ideal choice for President, Governors, or other positions. Yet, they did not have the right intention in their hearts. They were not a true nationalist. All they wanted was to spread their form of ideology. But it was not even about the ideology; they were not putting Brazil first. They were too busy maintaining their image in front of the international community that they forgot their first responsibility were the people who elected them. I am glad that Brazil and many countries in the world are choosing nationalist politicians to lead their countries.

So what is making Nationalism popular today?

# Nationalist Movement around the World

Many societies don't understand the true meaning of Nationalism. They think Nationalism will isolate their nation, which is why Nationalism can have a strained relationship with society's different norms. When a leader chooses Nationalism's path, they have to work harder to understand their country should always come first. There are prime examples of nations that have utilized Nationalism with the utmost success. Still, a country whose leader follows a nationalist ideology can face many problems from the global community. The reason behind this is simple. The global community might not be on the same page as a nationalist country.

The country's economic growth is one of the responsibilities of a nationalist leader. It should not be the only responsibility, though. Many nations think if a country chooses the path of Nationalism, they might not prosper, be isolated, and other countries might break diplomatic relations with them. On the other hand, there might be countries that have similar interests and the same nationalist values.

One of the prime examples of a nationalist country is the Meiji dynasty of Japan. During that time, the country went through enhanced development and expanded its territories. Even though the Japanese were known as cruel and unjust leaders in their control territories, the development they did to those countries led to the foundation of them being one of the most developed nations of their time. Countries like Korea and

Taiwan, which used to be Japanese colonies, adopted the Japanese modernization mindset, which brought development and economic stability to their countries. They also adopted the Japanese anti-communism stance, which got them the United States support, which was beneficial for the two countries. And by the 1970s, they both had started to adapt grassroots movement, a nationalism movement that gives the citizen of a particular country, in this case, Taiwan and Korea, more economical and political freedom. As a result, they prospered.

Two of the most populated countries also benefitted because of the nationalist movement. They were India and China. Even though their ideologies were left-leaning that brought them to odds with the United States, China benefitted from the nationalist revolution. The movement was more aligned with the general population than the nationalist revolution that shook Europe and other countries. Both nations learned from the mistakes made by other nationalist states and applied a carefully laid plan for their development.

Economic growth and the reason behind this was the equal justice system that helped citizens from society's different norms, leaving the younger generation demanding a political system change. Nationalism has played an important role in Turkish society; ever since the collapse of the Ottoman Empire, Mustafa Kemal Ataturk, the then leader of Turkey and its modern-day founder, tried to bring in nationalism reforms, starting with the Turkish language. He wanted to get rid of any foreign influence in the language itself. He also promoted pro-Turkish ideologies, in which Turkey came first.

Kemalism was an ideology founded by Mustafa Kemal Ataturk, in which Ataturk wanted to develop his nation for the future generations of the country. Ataturk implemented this in the Turkish ideology through a revolution, whose aim was to make a society where every religion and race could live in harmony. In the 1930s, Kemalism became the main policy of the Turkish constitution. It was decided that Turkey's entire state will follow the ideology, and it would remain the same as Ataturk.

Another primary example of Nationalism can be related to the United States ex-president, Donald Trump's first American slogan. Although, Donald Trump was not the only president who wanted to make American first as a part of the United States foreign policy. Woodrow Wilson used it during World War One to tell the world that the United States will not intervene in the war and remain neutral. But as I mentioned, Nationalism also had its side effects. That is isolation from the international community, which was one of Donald Trump's major problems when he wanted to implement the America First ideology into the country's foreign policy.

For Brazil, however, it is beneficial. Nationalism could benefit a country like Brazil as Brazil has seen its share of leaders who did not put the nation's interest first.

## Why Nationalist Parties Are the Ideal Choice for Brazil

The Nationalist Movement is spreading at a rapid speed worldwide. It is becoming more popular in many countries. Like in Europe, Austria and Hungary have nationalist leaders. Apart from India and China, the United States also had a nationalist leader, though he lost the elections to Joe Biden, a Centralist. Whereas, in Brazil, we have Jair Bolsonaro, who is a nationalist.

Like Bolsonaro, when Donald Trump was in power, he had one of the biggest political parties supporting him, the Republican Party. Alternatively, when Bolsonaro came into power, his party was just a middleweight party whose only role was gaining a few parliamentary seats in the Brazilian Congress. No one thought they could win the general election, and one of its candidates would become the President of Brazil. I am referring to Brazil's Social Liberal Party, whose name wasn't known by the international community before the 2018 general elections. But what made Brazilians chose this Nationalist political Party.

The reason is simple. They were tired of all the lies, corruption, the high level of crimes, and the declining economy done by Brazil's Workers Party. Bolsonaro, on the other hand, was kind of an outsider, and so was the social Liberal Party. The social Liberal Party strongly condemns the corruption done by the Workers Party. All the 52 elected deputies joined the cause, called "bullet," which encourages police to counter the rising crime rate. The party even has 16 Federal deputies who have experience with the Law Enforcement force and the Armed Forces. Even the Brazilian President Jair Bolsonaro and Vice President Hamilton Mourao used to be members of the Armed forces, with Bolsonaro being an ex-army captain and Hamilton

Mourao being an army general. Hence, these people united with the ideology of Brazil first.

Another thing that attracted a huge voter's base for the nationalist party was that they had made Brazil's first prime policy. Brazilians wanted a leader who would understand their problem. Brazilians wanted a leader, and most importantly, a party that would put Brazil first. Bolsonaro and the Social Liberal Party are doing exactly that.

When the whole world was locking down their countries because of the COVID-19 crisis, Brazil was not locking down its businesses. It was not going to close down its economy, and the reason behind that was not just Jair Bolsonaro but also his political Party. Bolsonaro decided against it because he thought the Brazilian economy was already in bad shape before the pandemic. If he had closed down the country, people would have lost their jobs and businesses, which would have made them lose their income source, which would have damaged an already fragile economy. He identified the chain reaction and stopped it from taking place.

That was just the start of Brazil's first policy. They even started to hand out money to those badly affected by the pandemic and the economic crisis. This made the party voter's base stronger. They even managed to influence Workers Party-dominated areas. That is the reason why a nationalist party is an ideal choice for Brazil. However, the problem is that when people hear about a nationalist party, their first thought is that it must be a Far-Right Nationalist Party. That is not the case as some countries prefer Left-wing nationalist political parties.

Confused about a left-wing and right-wing party? Well, let me break it down for you:

## The difference between Right-Wing populism and Left-Wing populism

Those who follow Right-Wing populism are nationalists and idealists, usually those who put their country first. As mentioned above, Woodrow Wilson was a nationalist leader who placed America first by not interfering in World War One. They are different in their ideologies and their approach to various social issues against the existing policies.

Left-Wing Populism, also known as social populism, is an ideology that usually involves left-wing politics and a populist theme. Those who follow Left-Wing populism are against the government. They try to support ordinary citizens and speak against social injustice that could be happening in their country. Their ideologies are different from Right-Wing populism.

Now let's look at the difference between Right and Left-Wing populism.

### Right-Wing Populism

**Conservative**: Political parties or politicians who follow Right-Wing populism tend to be more conservative. They will always oppose changes happening in the country that could harm that country's traditional values.

**Low Tax:** The government might allow businesses subsidies in the tax they have to pay. The government may be more lenient on the way a business conducts its business.

**Civil Rights:** Right-Wing political parties usually do not interfere with civil rights or other issues that have to do with its citizen. This is because they want to give their citizens more freedom to make their own decisions without the government or local administration interfering.

**Ideologies:** Right-Wing populism believes in an authoritarian reign, traditions, and Nationalism, where the country always comes first. They always tend to follow their tradition. Sometimes for the government to maintain this, they will be more authoritarian than the Left-wing populist Party.

## Left-wing Populism

**Approach:** Left-Wing populists might be more liberal in their approach to certain things happening in the country.

**Economy Policies:** Left-Wing populists want to make income equal for everyone regardless of sex, race, or religion. They also tend to have the tax increased for big corporations or wealthy individuals to use that money on other social causes.

**Government Role:** Left-Wing parties believe that the government should play a more active role in ordinary citizens' lives. They believe this will make the bond between the citizen and the government stronger.

**Ideology:** Left-Wing ideologies focus on equality, development, and the social development of their citizens. They are also looking to make reforms to the country's constitution to be more aligned with the current situation.

Spain is seeing the left-wing nationalist parties gaining ground in the general and local elections in recent years. This is because Podemos, a left-wing party, won only 8% of the votes in the 2014 European parliamentary elections.

In the 2015 general elections, they won 20.65% of the votes, making it the third-highest political party. Even in the current Spanish administration, there are people from the Left-wing political parties. One of them is Podemos Pablo Iglesias, the Deputy Prime Minister of Spain and Minister for Social Rights. So the nationalist movement, whether it is left or right, is on the right.

Having understood the difference, let's discuss Brazil's nationalism stance and what it means for Brazil.

## Brazilian Nationalism

Brazilian Nationalism is the ideology that combines the Brazilian people with its culture. It played an important part in the 19th century when Brazil declared its independence from the Portuguese empire. The reason behind the Brazilian nationalist movement was Portugal, as Brazil was its former colony. Many White-Brazilians got fed up with the Portuguese administration in Brazil and started to voice their support for independence. Even though the nationalist movement took place in the 19th century, it wasn't something new in the country, as it had been around since the 17th century.

Because of the Nationalist movement, the Portuguese administration in Brazil collapsed, and Brazil received its independence. However, even though Brazil got its independence, its nationalist movement didn't stop. It started to become an anti-British and anti-Spain stance that started to gather momentum in other countries.

Many people even started to speak French instead of Portuguese, which was the start of the growing anti-Portugal sentiment shared by many Brazilians. There was another reason for using the French Language. France was considered one of the most developed countries in the world. The Brazilians have a vision of making Brazil another France. When the Nationalist movement first emerged during the independence, many Brazilian united against the Portuguese administration and the political elites like the royal family. Farmers, slaves, and a lot of people united together.

That is also where the problem started as many elite-class accepted the rule of the Brazilian royal family. They were afraid that the slaves would start a revolution because they were in the majority. Hence, the elite class encouraged European citizens to migrate to Brazil so that the White-Population could have a majority against the slaves coming from Africa.

That is how Brazilian Nationalism first emerged. But who was the person who inspired the Brazilian nationalist Party to take the central stage? Who made Jair Bolsonaro the nationalist President of Brazil?

It was Olavo de Carvalho, who is also considered to be the man behind Jair Bolsonaro.

# The Man who inspired Brazilian Nationalism

For some people, Olavo de Carvalho can be a controversial figure. He is famous for his outspoken remarks about certain social norm topics. Still, Olavo de Carvalho is something else entirely. He is also known as Olavo in Brazil. He used to be an astrologist, communist, and journalist. And in recent times, he has become one of the most outspoken critics of the Brazilian Left-Wing Party, especially the Workers Party. Thousands hear his views on YouTube and Facebook. He is considered a hero by Brazil's Far-Right parties and a villain by the extremist left-wing political parties. His ideologies and anti-communist comments are broadcasted and discussed daily in Brazil, whether on Radio, Twitter, or some local newspaper and magazine.

Olavo is also the man whose ideologies have inspired Jair Bolsonaro. Olavo is also considered the architect behind Bolsonaro's power. When Bolsonaro visited the United States for the first time, he had dinner at the Brazilian ambassador's residence in the United States. Olavo was sitting beside Jair Bolsonaro, and when Bolsonaro said that he wanted to get rid of the country of the Left-Wing Parties, he gave credit for his victory to Olavo.

Olavo was also invited to an event hosted by ex-president Donald Trump and was introduced to 100 conservatives by the White House Chief of Strategist. So for the Right-Wings parties, he is a beacon of hope against their fight with the Left-Wing parties.

I believe if one person's ideologies can shape the country for the betterment, then why not? I hope you realize how essential it is for people to learn the difference between the left-wing nationalist and the right-wing nationalist and how it can change our respective country's political system. For Brazil, Jair Bolsonaro is the perfect candidate as a nationalist leader who can bring us forward.

# Chapter 10: Industrialization

*"Corporatization is the descendant of industrialization." -*
*Serj Tankian*

If the world hadn't experience industrialization, the world would still be living in the past. It would not have known what corporations are. It would not have known what the true meaning of revolution is. It would not have to move forward in its thinking. What Serj Tankian said is the truth. Corporatization is the descendant of industrialization. Without industrialization, we wouldn't have jobs, education, and or the advancement of nations. President Jair Bolsonaro wants Brazil to prosper economically for its young generations to get a chance at proper education and for Brazil to progress with the world.

Years of injustice inflicted upon Brazilian industries by the previous administration has made the job of the current administration of Jair Bolsonaro tough. But he is trying to find a way to revive the industries. He is trying to bring back the Brazilian economy, which is the sixth-largest in the world, and one of the largest in the Americas.

To some people, it may be hard to believe that Brazil has the largest industries in the world, but then again, it's a conception set by the previous governments of Brazil. In my next point, I will be discussing more the different industries in Brazil.

# Different Industries in Brazil

Brazil ranked third best in the Americas when it comes to industries. Brazil's industrial sector started with abundant workshops in the early part of the 19th century and was based in Brazil's southeast region. The workshop's primary role was melting iron and metals, producing necessities for the market, like wool, towel, candles, soap, and many other items that were required by the local market.

All of these items were produced with slaves who were utilized workers. These workers were underpaid or were used as free labor. Furthermore, the Alves Branco tariff that was introduced in 1857 helped with the growth of the industrial sector, which was facilitated by capital investment. One of the oldest industries that benefited from capital investment was the textile industry, but it didn't last for long, as in 1890, it started to decline.

Things were no less than a rollercoaster for Brazil in terms of industrialization. From 1840 to 1860, Brazil's time to shine came. Brazil saw its industries growing faster as Brazil started to produce the world's top quality products, and in large quantities, like fabric and fiber.

Additionally, the Brazil Industrial Association was established in 1880. Its creation was proof that Brazilian industries were enhancing rapidly. Today, Brazil's industries are the largest in the world. Brazil produces steel, coffee and is advancing in the technology sector as well. Most of the industries in Brazil are in the South and South-East regions.

Some of the different industries in Brazil are as follows: Automobile, Oil and Gas, Machinery and Equipment, Agriculture, Textile, and Coffee. Coffee happens to be Brazil's main product.

These industries somehow seem to have been overshadowed by other regions recently. Therefore, I feel the need to revisit them to show that we are among the top producers in the world still.

## Textile Industry In Brazil

The textile industry is estimated at $63 billion and is one of the largest and oldest industries in Brazil. Brazil homes around over 30,000 factories that produce 9.5 million garments annually. The industry's labor is the second largest in Brazil, with over 1.5 million people working for the textile industry. Brazil is also one of the few countries that produce fiber, design it, and then reproduce it. Brazil ranks fifth-largest in terms of cotton, and not just this, it is also the second-largest producer of denim jeans.

The textile industry happens to be the one such industry that was worked on and focused on by all previous governments.

## Brazilian Coffee Industry

Brazil, along with Vietnam and Colombia, is one of the largest coffee producers, with over 30% of coffee being exported from Brazilian ports. That makes coffee production one of the vital parts of Brazil's economy. But that is not the only role of Brazilian coffee. Throughout the years, coffee has been an integral part of Brazilian history.

The coffee plant first came from Ethiopia, exported by French merchants in the early part of the 18th century. Throughout the year, coffee has also played a major part in the Brazilian stock market, with the coffee industry having a share of 10.2% in the year 2011. The coffee industry can be found in 13 states in Brazil, with the largest being in Sao Paulo, Rio de Janeiro, and Bahia.

## Agriculture Industry In Brazil

The agriculture industry has played an important part in the Brazilian economy and in the livelihood of Brazilians. Brazil is the world's largest agricultural country, with 7.3% revenue coming from agriculture exports, which accounts for Brazil's 14% GDP. It also has the largest number of employees, with 9.8% of Brazilians working in the agriculture sector. But it has a darker root in Brazil's history. When the country was still a Portuguese colony, many slaves used to work for free on farms that were owned by their colonial masters.

With time, the European settlers moved from agriculture towards plantations, where coffee was one of the products discovered. Apart from that, sugar, rice, and tobacco were discovered as well, along with poultry. Today, many Middle Eastern countries purchase poultry from Brazil.

# Iron And Steel Industry In Brazil

In the 20th century, the steel industry grew rapidly as it found support from the government. The Brazilian government wanted this particular sector to boost the future of the Brazilian economy. The steel industry hired 110,000 workers alone in the year 2014, which has since grown swiftly. In the year 2017, the Brazilian steel and metal industry exports were at $3.7 billion. In the year 2019, this industry accounted for 3% of the Brazilian economy. Gerdau SA is one of Brazil's largest steel producers, with over 20% of steel being produced by them. Vale Bear operates the Brazilian iron mines in Carajas, which has over 67% of iron produced in Brazil.

Now, Jair Bolsonaro has played an indispensable part in promoting these industries, which was the only reason he got elected in the first place. In the 2018 elections, after ex-president Dilma Rousseff's impeachment in 2016 and ex-president Michel Temer's term coming to a disastrous end, the Brazilian economy was on a downfall. That is what led the business community to support Jair Bolsonaro. He has promised to bring Brazil's economy back to its prime glory. Had it not been for the recent pandemic, COVID-19, Jair Bolsonaro would have succeeded.

Thankfully, our industries are coming to the rescue of the nation in critical times.

# Industries Helping Brazil Get Out of The Economic Crisis

During the term of ex-president Dilma Rousseff, Brazil's economy suffered a lot. The economy ended up going into recession. Then, ex-president Michel Temer didn't do a lot to improve it. That is where President Jair Bolsonaro founded the success that got him elected. He inked the economic crisis to the years of corruption done by the previous administration, especially the Workers Party administration led by ex-president Lula. Rousseff's successorship after Lula only facilitated the remaining destruction.

Brazil's industry adds 17.1% to the GDP annually, but the country's economy was shrinking rapidly. The Covid-19 pandemic is making things worst. It is important to understand that the Brazilian industrialist needs help from the current administration.

Brazil's government needs to cut taxes for local businesses. They need to bring in more investors from other countries, which is what Bolsonaro is doing. He has called his Indian counterpart, Narendra Modi, and asked him to encourage Indian businesses to invest in Brazil in the construction, railways, mining, and energy sectors. Bolsonaro has also requested other countries to invest due to its natural reserve, especially in the Amazon Rainforest. India has already invested $6 billion in numerous sectors.

The current Brazilian administration has lined up numerous economic policies that can help a lot because, after the 2016 recession, Brazil's economic growth was at 1.1%. In the year 2019, it slowed down, even more, going as low as 0.8%.) The Brazilian government is trying to develop a policy that can improve the country's pension reforms. If the Brazilian Congress passes this policy, it will help the economy grow by 2.4% in the coming years.

The Brazilian Public Debt is at 88%, which is the highest in the world as per IMF. Therefore, the Brazilian government needs to help the business community in finding a solution. For if the debt keeps rising, the prices of production and products in the local market will remain at an all-time high. Given the current circumstances, soon, the employment rate would start to increase as well if the government does nothing to combat it. And given the track record of previous administrations, it suffices to say only Jair Bolsonaro seems to be the one keen on resolving Brazil's plight.

As mentioned before, Jair Bolsonaro is trying to attract foreign investors. That should give a boost to the local business. However, if he wants to succeed, he needs to cut down on taxes for foreign investors. This will encourage foreign investors to capitalize on different sectors of the Brazilian economy.

As you can see, if the government and the business community work together, they can create more jobs, which will lead to the country's economic growth. In turn, more industries will be able to benefit from funds. They will be able to hire more people and offer products at a cheaper cost. Foreign investments can assist various sectors, including educational institutes and medical centers.

I believe if the government is to plan carefully and reduce taxation, it will increase future investments as well. If the country improves its economy, many Brazilian firms will bring their operations from other countries. This will, in return, improve the ties of the business community with the government. And that is the trust Brazilian businesses have in Jair Bolsonaro. The business community seems to have asked for the governments' support. Understanding the situation, Jair Bolsonaro has promised to improve the Brazilian businesses in hopes of securing Brazil's interest and future.

## Bolsonaro improving Businesses in Brazil

On the 28th of October 2018, Brazil elected President Jair Bolsonaro as their leader. They chose his Far-Right government over the Workers Party, known as PT in Brazil. The reason behind this was simple - PT was corrupt. They bought down the country's economy and were not doing anything for the business community. This made the business community, especially the business elites, abandon them and support Jair Bolsonaro, who has promised great assistance from his administration.

Many people might call Jair Bolsonaro a controversial figure. They might call him the worst guy Brazil has ever elected, but let me make one thing clear, he is the only guy that is not corrupt. Jair Bolsonaro's pro-business policies have made him famous among the business community. Bolsonaro can take his own sweet time bringing in the reforms, but he is one of the best choices out of the two. Besides, there is the lingering fear of the PT returning to power if the current administration fails.

During the term of ex-president Termer, many businesses suffered at the expanse of his policies, which focused on the elimination of fiscal spending. This would have enhanced the public spending sector, which would have been a good thing for some people. However, it would have damaged the market confidence, causing lesser people to invest in businesses. Consequently, it would result in the closure of many businesses in Brazil.

Furthermore, the Temer administration also overturned labor reforms, which viewed the unemployment rate as escalating, further damaging Brazil's economy and businesses. And the shift of the government policy towards the central bank dual mandate made businesses fear the government was interfering with monetary policy. That was why the PT Presidential candidate lost the 2018 general elections, as one of his plans was the move to the center. On the other hand, Jair Bolsonaro has introduced a more pro-market business plan to attract foreign investors to Brazil.

Right afterward, he was elected, the Brazilian currency grew more than 12%. This was all the proof that the business community needed. Bolsonaro's policies will support them and put their interest first.

Last year during the peak of COVID-19, where the governments were locking down their countries, closing their borders, and economies were being ruined in the process,

President Jair Bolsonaro decided to do the complete opposite. He told his government they would not be shutting down Brazil as it would damage an already fragile economy. His exact words were that people would lose their jobs and would die out of hunger. He even blamed several Brazilian governors who wanted to impose curfews in their states and were forcing Bolsonaro to do the same.

As mentioned earlier, Jair Bolsonaro wants to turn Brazil into an industrialization hub. He is trying to develop and maintain a healthy relationship with the local business community. That very business community supported Jair Bolsonaro over the Workers Party, also known as PT, in the 2018 General Elections. Businessmen were tired of the corruption conducted by the PT. The corruption PT was involved in has damaged the Brazilian economy to such great extent that reversing it seems year's worth of efforts.

## The Relationship between the Brazilian Business Community and the Current Administration

The relationship between a leader and the business community must be strong in any country as these two sectors are the most powerful institutions. If the government bodies and business communities stand together like a pillar, they can lift their country. And that is what Brazilian's did in the election of 2018. The business elites supported President Jair Bolsonaro, though it was nothing new. After all, the Brazilian business elites have been trying to influence the local government since 2002.

First, it was ex-president Lula, and then it was his protégée ex-president, Rousseff. Apart from them, ex-president Michel Temer was no exception in the list of people who have given corruption a boost. However, these people came to power because of the support of the Brazilian business community. Nevertheless, the problem started when these politicians started to violate the trust of the business community.

President Lula was the one to have started with corruption. Soon enough, Rousseff and then Michel Temer followed in Lula's footsteps. They started abusing their power, which forced the business community to shift their allegiance from the far-left to the far-right. It didn't even take them long because, in less than ten years, the business community was leaning towards a politician who wasn't new, though his clean record earns him the title of being new.

When Bolsonaro came into power in 2018 via the general elections, he picked up 55% of the votes. There were many reasons behind this. Many Brazilians were jobless as the economy had taken a turn for the worst. Even the previous administrations' attempts had failed to recover the Brazilian economy. The previous government's failures frustrated the business community. The economic crisis caused a rapid rise in street crimes, murders, and all sorts of law-breaking on the streets. This finally bought the business community together. They decided to fully support Jair Bolsonaro.

When the previous administrations of Michel Temer failed to revise pension reforms in the country, Jair Bolsonaro supported that the reforms were necessary if Brazil wanted to get off of its current crisis. The pension reform was one of the reasons behind the Brazilian currency dropping by more than 2% as Michel Temer failed to make changes in due time, which Bolsonaro changed after his term began in 2018.

The Brazilian economy was 3.6% from September until the following day when Jair Bolsonaro won. He caused an increase to 4.1%, making him earn the trust of the business community. They believed Jair Bolsonaro was the only one who could bring out Brazil from their current state.

Now, Jair Bolsonaro was doing just that; reforming policies to improve the Brazilian economy until Covid-19 hit the county. It brought many challenges, all of which were taking hits at a weak economy, which again frustrated the business community. The community assumed they would end up in the same situation as the previous administrations and started doubting Jair Bolsonaro's practices. They started to feel hopeless again, and this was a feeling that they were too familiar with. Lula was the only one who made Brazilian's feel vulnerable and doubtful.

## How Lula Broke the Business Community Trust

As Brazil incurred a hit at the expanse of COVID-19, Brazilian's started to look back at all the destruction brought about by previous politicians.

When Lula was elected in 2002, it was a turning point in Brazilian history. The country had elected a leader who used to be a factory worker. Lula was a leader who brought hope that he would be different, he won't be a tyrant, and he would try to change the country for the better. Although, Brazilian's couldn't have been more wrong.

The first sign was that the business community didn't like a left-wing politician taking over the public office, and that made them back away from Lula. The business body refused to support Lula or any of his policies. That is when Lula made the business community a counteroffer, for if he hadn't done so, the economy would have collapsed without any means to salvage it.

Lula was offering the business community a promise of stability and financial reforms if they would work with his administration.

This little scenario that was taking place in Brazil took everyone by surprise. Both the international community and locals were surprised. A strong alliance was forming between Lula's government and the powerful business associations. And that was only the start of what we know as the Brazilian economic growth.

Lula's economic development policy was known as "New Developmentalism." It was a good thing as it meant to support multinational corporations by providing them low-interest loans from the local banks. Soon enough, many political analysts started calling this policy by another name. That was "FIESP Agenda," also known as Brazil's most powerful business association, named the Federations of Industries of Sao Paulo. Again, it started to shift the countries opinion towards Lula, making people believe he was working with the business community to create a better future.

That illusion of a better tomorrow, however, was short-lived. Even though the business community enjoyed their close relationship with Lula, Lula launched another policy called the "Bolsa Familia." It was a good policy as it aimed to provide financial assistance to less-privileged families. The only thing that Lula's administration was asking in return was for parents to send their children to school at all costs. Sounds like Nirvana, right?

The policy was an instant boost injected into the Brazilian economy. The standard of living improved significantly. Salaries increased, making locals change their lifestyles. It also helped increase the population of middle-class families. Inequality was diminishing. Several local businesses expanded their operations, even globally. Alas! As glad tidings came, they were only shadowing the storm that was about to hit Brazil.

Everyone thought Lula was going to change the economy. He was doing it, but then something went wrong. Lula made a huge mistake by violating the trust of the business community by picking his protégée, Rousseff. as the next president. She did a horrible job. She caused the economy to plunge once again despite the success of the 2014 FIFA world cup.

In 2016, the country, for the first time in its history, hosted the 2016 summer Olympics. Alternatively, as good happened, so did bad. While the country was successfully hosting international events, corruption scandals appeared. Operation

Car Wash came to the attention of the public and the international community. Brazilians felt backstabbed by Lula. He had promised them a good economy, a good future, gave an illusion of betterment so that no one would find out what he was doing behind their back. Lula managed to do so with the help of Rousseff. Rousseff was impeached. The man who betrayed her, Michel Temer, was the worst, with an approval rating of less than 6%, and soon after, Lula was sent to prison.

Lula may have started on the right track, but greed led to his downfall. We need to understand why it is important to select our leaders wisely. What they choose to do during their term directly impacts us as a whole.

I hope you find out why the Far-Right, Jair Bolsonaro, is a far better option for Brazil's future now. Not only is Bolsonaro void of corruption, but he also wants to bring industrialization to the country. He wants to see the country flourish. He wants the country to move forward. We need to understand that, at times, our leaders are as powerless as anyone else in front of natural disasters and widespread illnesses. What matters is how they are working to combat the situation.

The COVID-19 is a pandemic. Lula might have seemed like the ideal choice, but in the end, he was a tyrant in the making who only cared about himself. At the same time, Bolsonaro has proven himself to be the opposite. Let's try not to tie down Bolsonaro to the setbacks brought forward by the Coronavirus. After all, it is not like Brazil has another choice. Would we rather make the same mistake twice? Or give someone else a chance?

# Chapter 11: The Young People

*"We all understand that compromise is part of the legislative process, yet at the same time, I would submit that wilderness is not for sale." -**Nick Rahall***

Legislative is a system created to lead the country towards a brighter future. It is the fundamental duty of every citizen to pick the right choice, a choice based on the right ideology for the country. This choice is supposed to be the perfect plan for a brighter future of that country, to have someone to make the right choices. But as Nick Rahall said, "sometimes the politicians we choose to represent us in the upper house, and the lower house of legislative have to make compromises, which we call democracy."

Now, let's look at all of those countries that allow their citizens to pick their legislative bodies. By doing so, those countries allow their citizens to have a voice that can change the country's dimension. India and China are two of the biggest countries in the world. They are two of the largest economies, with an army and a huge population. Still, there is something that separates them. While India is the biggest democracy globally, with elected bodies that their citizens choose, China has taken this crucial right from their citizens.

This is because China is afraid that if it allows its citizens to choose the leader, it will lose its ideology. That's the difference between India and China. India has shown they are a democracy that can shape the world, which has positively impacted Brazil.

Brazil has given Bolsonaro his biggest challenge since he was elected, and that was the legislative elections in February of 2021.

## Legislative Elections of Brazil 2021

Jair Bolsonaro's challenge was his government being legislatively elected on the 1st of Feb 2021. That was a challenge that the President chose with all his might because he wanted to prove to the Brazilian public that they had made the right decision. This was his biggest challenge. Bolsonaro wanted to make sure he was on the right track. Most Brazilians thought of him as two of his allies had won this year's legislative elections. That has re-ignited hope for Jair Bolsonaro for next year's elections.

This result was essential for Jair Bolsonaro, as he was already facing 61 probes for impeachment. Because of that, he had a fragile relationship with the Brazilian Congress. When his allies won the elections, he showed his gratitude by posting a picture of himself with the two new congressional leaders to lead the country forward. Bolsonaro made sure he supported Arthur Lira for President of the Deputies, which is the lower house of the Brazilian Congress. Additionally, Rodrigo Pacheco is the newly elected President of the Senate. These two will be Bolsonaro pillars that will ensure Jair Bolsonaro passes the right bills beneficial for Brazil.

Irrespective of how things are at present, it will be a problem when young people, who Jair Bolsonaro is aiming to attract, are interested in socialist parties. Brazil is not alone in this. Many countries are reporting that their younger generations are attracted to Socialism.

## Why Young People Prefer Socialism over Capitalism and Nationalism

In the 19th century and the 20th century, the word socialism was very common. It was a word used positively...Nobody would have minded. When people discussed Socialism among friends and supported it, those around them would have supported Socialism. Still, as time went along, the word became nothing short of a taboo. It became a forbidden word when spoken in front of friends. People realized it was wrong. But there was a seed of Socialism that was still growing among a group of people. That group was supposed to be the backbone of a country. They are a group that is the future of any country, and that group is the students, the young generation.

The reason the youth is crazy about Socialism is because of one man. A man is planning to become the President of one of the most powerful countries in the world. He was Bernie Sanders, a democratic party senator planning on becoming the President of the United States on two occasions.

1) 2016, where he was not chosen as a nomination by his party.

2) 2020, when he lost the party position to becoming the country's President.

During the 2016 United States elections, many people were afraid as Bernie Sanders was a socialist. No one could even imagine a socialist man leading their country.

The United States has recently seen two congress members being elected who are openly socialist. When the local government took a survey, it showed signs that more than 70% of millennials would be satisfied with a socialist leader leading their country.

The reason behind this is simple. The youth are tired of the capitalist leaders playing with the country's economy. The youth don't understand their parent's problem with socialism, communism, or anything related to the far-left or even leaning slightly to the left? A research carried out with the United States Think Tank came up with a quick survey. They found out that more than 25% of people from the age group of 18 to 40 will be voting for a socialist leader if they are given a chance. The percentage gets smaller when it gets to 60 to 70 years old as this population is only 10%.

Let us take a quick peek at the year 2010, which was the root cause for the change of opinion in the young people's minds when it comes to favoring a socialist leader. In some states, the poll was tied, with half the population supporting a capitalist or nationalist leader and the other half supporting a socialist leader. In 2019, the poll again surveyed the young population, inquiring about their opinion on six different economies, including socialism, capitalism, major business corporations, small or start-up businesses free-enterprise. This time, despite socialism having a higher number of supporters, more than 80% of people supported a free market.

The voters were not satisfied when it came to big corporations, as their support was below 40%. But when it came to start-up companies and small businesses, many young voters had a positive response, with more than 95% supporting it. This has shown that young people are starting to change their ideologies in the United States, which can lead to many problems for the whole world as this has been the case for many people.

The youth is attracted to socialism because they aren't aware of its impact or consequences. Young people need to learn more about socialism and communism. They have to find out why it is not a suitable choice. Young people need to learn about the ideology behind communism and socialism.

## Young People Need to Learn About Socialism and Communism

Young people need to learn more about communism and Socialism and not consider it cool or something that can change their lives for the better.

Brazil trusted a guy who was thought to be a perfect choice. He was someone everyone considered a hero. He is someone I have mentioned numerous times in this book. Yes, I am talking about ex-president Lula, though Brazil was not the only country that mistook a real leader's ideologies.

Italy has seen its government changing at a very rapid pace. They have moved from left-wing to far-right through the years. They had seen the Italian Socialist Party, famously known as PSI, come into power in 1983 when Bettino Craxi led it. Bettino tried to mend the country's economic crisis with other socialist parties' help.

Even though Bettino cut off all links with the Soviet Union, which goes against all the traditions of his parties, Bettino Craxi maintains a good relationship with other socialist leaders in Europe. He is also the de-facto leader of the socialist movement that hit Europe in the 1990s. Still, if the young people look at these from another point of view, they will realize something that did change...How the rest of the world saw Italy.

Bettino was not favored by countries that did not support Socialism, as Bettino was a man who supported socialist groups in Europe and beyond. He even supported socialist groups fighting their government in Uruguay. Bettino even refused to hand over the United States cruise ship hijacked by the hijackers. He even promised to hand the hijackers over to the US, but at the last moment decided to give the hijackers safe passage to another country. His act severely damaged Italy and United States' relationship. If young people look at all of this, they will realize what Bettino's method was, as it isolated Italy from the rest of the world.

Young people need to study Socialism and its policies in-depth before deciding to elect a socialist leader as their President. Look at Cuba. They have a socialist leader, and they didn't even get the chance to choose him. He just came in one day and took over the power. Cubans have to live under the rule of a tyrant, but Cuba is not the only country with a dictator.

Look at North Korea. They have one of the worst leaders in the world. The reason behind this is simple; Socialism takes away the power of freedom of speech. It takes away your freedom to vote. Hence, I am repeating - Young people have to study Socialism.

## In Hindsight

I have discussed the basic concept behind communism and how it has changed the world. We have talked about how people should tackle communism. When people wonder if this can work, they should look at the Soviet Union. The USSR was considered one of the world's most powerful countries. It was a country that had spread its ideologies throughout the world, including Germany, Vietnam, China, Mexico, Cuba, Brazil, Argentine, Colombia, and even tried to influence the United States with their fake ideology. In the end, however, they failed. The USSR collapsed.

I have also discussed Jair Bolsonaro, the current President of Brazil, and how he is trying to help clean up the country that was sinking in corruption, crime, economic crisis, and years of mistrust at the expense of previous governments. That clean-up comprises acts done by the Workers Party of Brazil, which was also one of the topics we discussed. When I was talking about Cuba in the point above, I referred to one of the chapters in this book. Yes, that chapter is the one where I discussed democracy and dictatorship. Cuba is a country that was ruled by a dictator who was trying to spread his fake ideologies. He even corrupted Brazil when the country was ruled by a left-wing politician, which almost destroyed Brazil from within.

This leads to the part where I discussed why the bilateral relationship is essential for a country. It is the leader's priority to make sure their country has a positive image in front of the international community. It is crucial other countries respect yours, especially internal matters. Else, with the unwanted involvement of other countries, the risk of war will increase, and disputes will erupt.

We have discussed how Bolsonaro is viewed as a nationalist leader, how he is changing Brazil, and how he is developing the industrial sector of Brazil. Despite facing heavy criticism from the international community, especially from the French President, he continues to stand his ground. They blame him for burning the Amazon rainforest. Still, Jair Bolsonaro is trying to do what is best for the country.

## Communism is a Failure in a Country Like Brazil

The left-wing parties got their shot in changing how Brazilians view them. They have a chance of changing the mind of young voters, business elites, the international community, and political rivals. That is because when a leader is doing something good for the country, the opposition respects them as well. It was something that the left-wing leaders did not do; Lula and Rousseff were busy doing things that benefitted them and not the country in general.

With time, people realized what they did was wrong. The people realized that communism/socialism, whatever name the left-wing parties give to their fake ideologies, was leading Brazil towards a darker path, towards a path that was going to isolate them. And the realization came when Brazil woke up to the Operation Car Wash scandal, which shook Brazil's political elites.

Many of the country's top politicians, businessmen, and top government officials were arrested on corruption charges. That made Brazil choose a leader who changed the Brazilian political landscape.

The people decided to give Bolsonaro a chance as their president. He is a man who is not corrupt, a man who is not from the political elites, a man who is deemed unfit for the presidential office. Yet, he is the right choice as Brazilians wanted a man who thinks outside of the box, who would take them out of their current economic crisis, high crime rate, and internal problems. Jair Bolsonaro is the most suitable man for Brazil. He is a man who will defeat the left-wing parties in next year's general elections. He is a man who is doing exactly what he promised.

# Chapter 12: Sete de Setembro

*"For to be free is not merely to cast off one's chains, but to live in a way that respects and enhances the freedom of others."*
**Nelson Mandela**

7th September, a day that has become a symbol of freedom, was a day that people could choose which path was suitable for them. When we hear the discussion about freedom, we usually discover that each of us has a different opinion. Some think that freedom is freedom of speech, but that has been misused in societies around the world to target the weak, the oppressed. Then some want freedom for religion, which has always been one of the controversial topics. Those topics have caused riots to erupt, but at the same time, we cannot deny the fact that it is also the root cause for many countries gaining independence. But there is something that many of us want: freedom to choose, freedom to breathe, and freedom to do what is right.

7th September might be another date of the year for some people. Still, it is a day of celebration; it is a day when families come together and remember the past; when Grandparents tell their grandchildren and their children about their struggles, it is a day of independence. Let me tell you now what happened on this date not too long ago, and maybe it was a day that will never be forgotten because many of us took a stand against the tyrant who wanted to bring us back to a time where there was no freedom.

## The Protest That Changed It All

Brazil's President Jair Bolsonaro has been encouraging his followers to march in the streets for months. So, on 7th September, Brazil's Independence Day, there were unconfirmed reports that Bolsonaro planned to mobilize mobs of armed citizens in yellow-and-green jerseys, several of them wearing furry hats and carrying trumpets, trying to storm the Supreme Court building — Brazil very own imitation of the Capitol riot,— well, that is what the Opposition wanted the people to believe, they wanted to print a negative image of the president, they want to make him look like an oppressor when he wants to do what is right for the people.

That, thankfully, was not the case. "Eventually, the protesters dispersed, and no one attempted to sit in the Supreme Court judges' chairs." Brazilians, on the other hand, were not spared the confusion and anxiety. It was a show of strength for Mr. Bolsonaro. He said he planned to utilize the size of the gathering as an "ultimatum for everybody" in the three different branches of the government in the morning, speaking to a crowd of roughly 3 million people in Brasilia. In the run-up to the protest, the president dubbed the upcoming elections in 2022 "a farce" and claimed he would no longer abide by Supreme Court justices' orders at a 125,000-strong gathering in Sao Paulo. He said, "I'm letting the crooks know that I'll never be arrested!"

President Jair Bolsonaro spoke to supporters on the eve of the Sete de Setembro holiday, also known as "Independence Day," during a big rally on Avenida Paulista in São Paulo. Bolsonaro supposedly condemned the STF minister, Alexandre de Moraes, the Court, and the electoral system, contrary to what he said that morning in Brasilia. Protests erupted in Rio de Janeiro, Brasil, and other Brazilian cities, in response to the capital of Sao Paulo. Bolsonaro told the demonstrators that he would no longer "acknowledge that criminals like Alexandre de Moraes continue to tear our democracy and violate our Constitution."

"To remind this minister that there is still time for him to change his ways. He still has time to complete his investigations. Stop becoming a thug and hurting the Brazilian people, says Alexandre de Moraes "he also added. Still on Moraes, the president stated that he might not follow the minister's recommendations and urged the release of "political prisoners," referring to his supporters who have been the subject of recent indictments in the so-called "inquiry into undemocratic conduct."

Jair Bolsonaro has again advocated for election reform in Brazil, describing the current race as a "sham." "We cannot accept an electoral system that provides no protection during elections. We want transparent, democratic elections with open vote counting and auditable voting. I cannot participate in a sham like this, which is still being supported by the head of the Superior Electoral Court. "He made some changes in the way he delivered his message.

*"Life without liberty is like a body without spirit."Kahlil Gibran*

"To those who seek to make me unfit in Brasilia, only God can bring me out of there," Bolsonaro stated at the conclusion of his speech, once again adding that he will never be imprisoned. Jair Bolsonaro talked on top of a sound truck for roughly 20 minutes before leaving, "To those who seek to make me unfit in Brasilia, only God can bring me out of there," Bolsonaro stated at the conclusion of his speech, once again adding that he will never be imprisoned. Jair Bolsonaro talked on top of a sound truck for roughly 20 minutes before leaving Avenida Paulista a few moments later. Demonstrators in support of the President blocked the two lanes of traffic at the location. Since 9 a.m on the independence day, the area was closed in both directions.

Before actually going to the protest, the President flew in from Rio de Janeiro and was accompanied by officials such as Onyx Lorenzoni "Labour and Social Security," Tarcisio Freitas "Infrastructure," Milton Ribeiro "Ministry of Education," Carlos Alberto França "Foreign Affairs," he was also accompanied by Luiz Eduardo Ramos "General Secretariat," Bruno Bianco "General Attorney of the Union," and Deputy Eduardo Bolsonaro "PSL-SP." It was a way for President Bolsonaro to show his supporters, those closest to him, his closest of ministers were there for him in this tough time and that they were a united force that would bring Brazil out of any problem that it faces. In another protest that day, Jair Bolsonaro gave an address, which was delivered on the promise of reiterating the morning speech in Brasilia. Bolsonaro reiterated his call for "unreasonable demand to all of the Praça dos Três Poderes," throughout the gathering. "Any legislation, action, or sentence that goes beyond the four lines of the Constitution will no longer be accepted," he declared.

In Sao Paulo, demonstrations against the President's administration drew a smaller crowd than the president supporters in the Anhangabau Valley, just four kilometers from where Bolsonaro's supporters gathered. Another group of president supporters held a parade that morning in Ponte Estacada, south of Sao Paulo. The security arrangement in the Brazilian capital of Sao Paulo was beefed up, but the protests were calm for most of the day. Nevertheless, just as a precaution, the metro station, Trianon–Masp, was shut down.

## Protest Spread Across The Country During The Independence Day Celebration

All through the morning, pro-President protest movements did take place in the nation's major cities. There was no evidence of any conflicts. Protests against the administration were held on the morning of the celebration but in lower numbers. The largest protests were held in Sao Paulo, Brasilia, and Rio de Janeiro. Other capitals, such as Salvador, Belém, Curitiba, and Belo Horizonte, were also listed as protest site. The Avenida Atlântica in Rio de Janeiro was one of the first protests at about 9 a.m. on independence day. The avenue's three lanes were all occupied. This showed the president supporters that he was a man who would not bow down to the corrupt judicial system, that he would not stop standing up to those who wanted to portray a negative image of the president. He would never accept a loss when he is trying to do something that no other president in history has done to make brazil corruption-free. Overall there were 30 million people that took to the streets on independence day; this was a record for this country; this showed that despite the polls showing that Bolsonaro will lose next year's election, he still has a strong following. He may surprise his rivals, such as ex-president Lula da Silva.

I hope you realize that if a leader sets his mind to liberating his nation from the corrupt, the vile, the tyrant, he will always have the support of the people; he will always win. With that, he can face anything that is thrown his way. You know something when Brazil gained its independence, it wasn't through the brute force, no, it wasn't through invading another country, it wasn't through terrorist strategist, no it was through diplomatic talks with different world power of that time, and that is what Jair Bolsonaro is trying to do, he doesn't want to use brute force against the opposition, even though many media outlets are labeling him as a tyrant leader who wants to use the military to seize power, but that is not true. He also doesn't want to cause people to suffer; he wants to make his rivals understand that he will not lose the elections without a fight.

Some words taken from signs on the demonstration, held on by the people in Boston, on September six, 2021:

– TSE, why afraid of the printed vote?

- our freedom of speech is under attack!

- Brazilians are being silenced by politicians that were not elected by us.

- Brazilian journalists and citizens are being jailed for having an opinion.

- BOLSONARO in 2022! Our freedom is our priority!

- judges if the Brazilian Supreme Court subverted the democracy

- Supreme is the people! An auditable and printed vote is what we want!

- we DEMAND auditable vote, with a public count, and the cleaning of our institutions.

- Brazilian justices are tearing apart our constitution

- our Brazilian flag will never be red

- in 2022, Brazil will see that your sons will never give up the fight!

- our democracy is at risk in Brazil; corrupts are being free, and journalists are being jailed.

As I come to the end of the book, I would like to thank you for enduring my thoughts. I thank you for following me on a journey that I hope will lead you towards the right path. I hope by now you realize that socialism and communism are the same things. If you are ever in doubt, look at the UK, they chose Boris Johnson as their Prime Minister instead of Jeremy Corbyn, a socialist leader of the Workers Party. They should take inspiration from people who have resisted dictators that have ruined their countries and other countries by spreading what we all know as fake ideologies.

Just consider this, you have to earn what you get in this life. And, socialism will give you that for free, but it will come at a great cost.

# References

## Chapter 1

Amadeo, Kimberly. "What Is Communism?" *The Balance*, 2021, https://www.thebalance.com/communism-characteristics-pros-cons-examples-3305589.

Pipes, Richard. "Soviet Union - Lenin's Disillusionment | Britannica." *Britannica*, https://www.britannica.com/place/Soviet-Union/Lenins-disillusionment. Accessed 3 May 2021.

Rosenberg, Matt. "A List of Current Communist Countries in the World." *ThoughtCo.*, 2020, https://www.thoughtco.com/communist-countries-overview-1435178.

## Chapter 2

Bevins, V. (2020). *Where Conspiracy Reigns*. The Atlantic. https://www.theatlantic.com/ideas/archive/2020/09/how-anti-communist-conspiracies-haunt-brazil/614665/

*Far-right Jair Bolsonaro wins Brazil's presidential election | News | DW | 28.10.2018*. (n.d.). DW. Retrieved May 3, 2021, from https://www.dw.com/en/far-right-jair-bolsonaro-wins-brazils-presidential-election/a-46065594

*"The Country That Saved Itself" | Brazil: Five Centuries of Change*. (n.d.). Retrieved May 3, 2021, from

https://library.brown.edu/create/fivecenturiesofchange/chapt
ers/chapter-7/clarence-hall/

## Chapter 3

*Bolsonaro called the biggest threat to Brazil's coronavirus response | Coronavirus pandemic News | Al Jazeera.* (2020). AlJazeera. https://www.aljazeera.com/news/2020/5/9/bolsonaro-called-biggest-threat-to-brazils-coronavirus-response

*Bolsonaro signs anti-crime bill designed to tackle violence in Brazil | Reuters.* (2019). Reuters. https://www.reuters.com/article/us-brazil-politics-anti-crime-idUSKBN1YT0MF

Child, D. (2019). *Who is Jair Bolsonaro, Brazil's new far-right president? | Elections News | Al Jazeera.* AlJazeera. https://www.aljazeera.com/news/2019/1/1/who-is-jair-bolsonaro-brazils-new-far-right-president

Gallas, D., & Palumbo, D. (2019). *What's gone wrong with Brazil's economy? - BBC News.* BBC News. https://www.bbc.com/news/business-48386415

Wallenfeldt, J. (2021). *Jair Bolsonaro | Biography & Facts | Britannica.* Britannica. https://www.britannica.com/biography/Jair-Bolsonaro

## Chapter 4

Araujo, F. (2018). *How Left Lost Brazil | The New Republic.* The New Republic. https://newrepublic.com/article/151082/left-lost-brazil

Cowie, S. (2018). *Bolsonaro wants to 'cleanse' Brazil of left-wing 'criminals' | Elections News | Al Jazeera.* AlJazeera. https://www.aljazeera.com/news/2018/10/23/bolsonaro-wants-to-cleanse-brazil-of-left-wing-criminals

*Jair Bolsonaro: Far-right candidate wins Brazil poll - BBC News.* (2018). BBC News. https://www.bbc.com/news/world-latin-america-46013408

## Chapter 5

Jon Lee, A. (2020). *In Brazil, Jair Bolsonaro, Trump's Close Ally, Dangerously Downplays the Coronavirus Risk | The New Yorker.* The New Yorker. https://www.newyorker.com/news/daily-comment/in-brazil-jair-bolsonaro-trumps-close-ally-dangerously-downplays-the-coronavirus-risk

Liptak, K. (2019). *Jair Bolsonaro fawns over Trump decries "fake news" - CNNPolitics.* CNN. https://edition.cnn.com/2019/03/19/politics/donald-trump-jair-bolsonaro-brazil-white-house/index.html

Reuters. (2019). *Bolsonaro: Brazil has been "liberated from socialism, political correctness."* NBC News. https://www.nbcnews.com/news/latino/bolsonaro-brazil-has-been-liberated-socialism-political-correctness-n953736

Setzler, M. (2021). Did Brazilians Vote for Jair Bolsonaro Because They Share his Most Controversial Views? *Brazilian Political Science Review*, *15*(1), 15. https://doi.org/10.1590/1981-3821202100010006

*Venezuela crisis: Brazil vows to deliver aid, defying Maduro - BBC News.* (2019). BBC News. https://www.bbc.com/news/world-latin-america-47300962

## Chapter 6

Bardhan, P. (2020). *The two largest democracies in the world are the sickest now.* Scroll. https://scroll.in/article/971086/the-two-largest-democracies-in-the-world-are-the-sickest-now

Chibba, M. (2020). *Political economy and democracy in Brazil under Bolsonaro / openDemocracy.* Open Democracy. https://www.opendemocracy.net/en/democraciaabierta/political-economy-and-democracy-brazil/

Dahl, R. (2021). *democracy / Definition, History, Meaning, Types, Examples, & Facts / Britannica.* Britannica. https://www.britannica.com/topic/democracy

## Chapter 7

Alvares, Debora. "Municipal Elections Highlight Challenges Facing Brazil's Left-Wing." *The Brazilian Report*, 2020, https://brazilian.report/power/2020/11/09/municipal-elections-highlight-challenges-facing-brazils-left-wing/.

"Amazon Fires: Brazil Sends Army to Help Tackle Blazes - BBC News." *BBC News*, 2019, https://www.bbc.com/news/world-latin-america-49452789.

"Brazil Corruption Scandals: All You Need to Know - BBC News." *BBC News*, 2018, https://www.bbc.com/news/world-latin-america-35810578.

Wilson, Stephanie J., et al. "Daily Spousal Responsiveness Predicts Longer-Term Trajectories of Patients' Physical Function." *Psychological Science*, vol. 28, no. 6, 2017, pp. 786–97, doi:10.1177/0956797617697444.

## Chapter 8

Bethell, Leslie. "Brazil as a Regional Power in Latin America or South America?" *SAIIA*, 2010, https://media.africaportal.org/documents/SAIIA_Policy_Briefing_no_13.pdf.

Milhorance de Castro, Carolina. "Brazil's South-South Foreign Policy Post-Lula | Cairn International Edition." *Cairn Info*, 2013, pp. 45–59, https://www.cairn-int.info/article-E_AFCO_248_0045--brazil-s-south-south-foreign-policy-post.htm#.

Russo, Guilherme. "How Brazilians View Their Country's Economic, Political Crises | Pew Research Center." *Pew Research Center*, 2017, https://www.pewresearch.org/fact-tank/2017/07/06/how-brazilians-view-their-countrys-economic-and-political-crises/.

Stuenkel, Oliver. "What Will the U.S. Election Mean for Brazil's Diplomacy?" *Foreign Policy*, 2020, https://foreignpolicy.com/2020/10/31/u-s-election-2020-stakes-brazil-bolsonaro-trump-biden-diplomacy-trade-climate-change/.

## Chapter 9

Duara, Prasenjit. "Development and the Crisis of Global Nationalism." *Brookings*, 2018, https://www.brookings.edu/blog/future-development/2018/10/04/development-and-the-crisis-of-global-nationalism/.

Duarte, Letícia. "Meet Olavo de Carvalho, Brazilian President Jair Bolsonaro's Inspiration - The Atlantic." *The Atlantic*, 2019, https://www.theatlantic.com/international/archive/2019/12/brazil-olavo-de-carvalho-jair-bolsonaro/604117/.

## Chapter 10

Carvalho, Laura. "How Did the Brazilian Economy Help to Elect Bolsonaro? | LSE Latin America and Caribbean." *LSE Blogs*, 2019, https://blogs.lse.ac.uk/latamcaribbean/2019/10/02/how-did-the-brazilian-economy-help-to-elect-bolsonaro/.

Chakraborty, Subhayan. "Brazilian President Bolsonaro Calls for Investments by Indian Companies | Business Standard News." *Business Standard*, 2020, https://www.business-standard.com/article/economy-policy/brazilian-president-bolsonaro-calls-for-investments-by-indian-companies-120012800080_1.html.

Lee, Alec. "What Businesses Should Know About Brazil's New President." *Harvard Business Review*, 2018, https://hbr.org/2018/12/what-businesses-should-know-about-brazils-new-president.

Mandl, Carolina, and Leonardo Benassatto. "Brazil's Bolsonaro Says Coronavirus Restrictions Kill Economy." *Reu*, 2020, https://www.reuters.com/article/us-health-coronavirus-brazil-idUSKCN24J0V8.

Sawe, Benjamin Elisha. "The Biggest Industries In Brazil." *World Atlas*, 2017, https://www.worldatlas.com/articles/which-are-the-biggest-industries-in-brazil.html.

# Chapter 11

"Brazil Congress Elects Bolsonaro Allies as New Leaders | Latin America News | Al Jazeera." *AlJazeera*, 2021, https://www.aljazeera.com/news/2021/2/2/brazil-congress-elects-bolsonaro-allies-as-new-leaders.

Chapman, Steve. "Why Millennials Are Drawn to Socialism - Chicago Tribune." *Chicago Tribune*, 2018, https://www.chicagotribune.com/columns/steve-chapman/ct-perspec-chapman-young-socialism-capitalism-20180520-story.html.

Hoffower, Hillary. "5 Facts That Explain Why 70% of Millennials Would Vote for a Socialist." *Business Insider*, 2019, https://www.businessinsider.com/millennials-would-vote-socialist-bernie-sanders-elizabeth-warren-debt-2019-10.

Sanders, Sam. "Why Do Young People Like Socialism More Than Older People Do?" *NPR*, 2015, https://www.npr.org/2015/11/21/456676215/why-do-young-people-like-socialism-more-than-older-people.

# Chapter 12

Vanessa Barbara,(2021), Bolsonaro Is Getting Desperate, and Its Clear What He Wants, Retrieve From https://www.nytimes.com/2021/09/15/opinion/bolsonaro-brazil-independence-day.html

(2021), Protesters Crowd Aveinda Paulista On A Day Of Storng Protest In The Capital, Retrieve From https://www.gazetadopovo.com.br/republica/manifestantes-lotam-avenida-paulista-confira-tarde-de-atos-pelo-brasil/

[1] Tim Vickery, (2021), Brazilians Stage Mass Rallies In Support Of Bolsonaro on Attack On Judiciary, Retrieve From https://www.youtube.com/watch?v=loFi3bJRAy4&t=41s

Made in United States
North Haven, CT
24 January 2022

15229280R00100